Lighting the Blue Touch Paper

A Handbook for Igniting the Energy, Clarity and Performance of Senior Leadership Team

Les Murray

Lighting The Blue Touch Paper:
A Handbook for Igniting Energy, Clarity and Performance in the Senior Leadership Team
©2025 20-20 Management Enterprise Ltd

ISBN: 9781919258805 Paperback

Published by: Inspired By Publishing

The strategies in this book are presented primarily for enjoyment and educational purposes. Every effort has been made to trace copyright holders and obtain their permission for the use of copyright material.

The information and resources provided in this book are based upon the authors' personal experiences. Any outcome, income statements or other results, are based on the authors' experiences and there is no guarantee that your experience will be the same. There is an inherent risk in any business enterprise or activity and there is no guarantee that you will have similar results as the author as a result of reading this book.

The author reserves the right to make changes and assumes no responsibility or liability whatsoever on behalf of any purchaser or reader of these materials.

Acknowledgements

There are many people to thank who have helped me along the way. In particular, those who have helped me to produce this book.

People I would like to thank for their positive influence, and for indulging me with their time, care and attention include: Barry Sealey, Bruce Giles, Edward R.S. Whitefield, Arnold Louw, Peter Moorhouse, Thomas Payne, Peter Grender, Martin Grant, John McKeown, Andy Stapley, Bill Gilmour, Kelvin Coyle, Saul Lanyado, John Paterson, Terry Stock, Rick Curtis, Tony Wood, Hans Haefeli, Mark Papworth, Bob Dabic and Paul Johnson. Each of you has left a far deeper and more lasting impression on me than you will ever know.

There are too many colleagues to highlight, but my special thanks for patience, learning and fun goes to Bob Gorrie, Chris Turner, Kevin Jones, Eamon Hegarty, Mike Lewkowicz, Amanda Poole, Mark Matthews, Antony Segrove, Martin Hersov, Philip Walker, Jeff Toig, Peter Williams, Andy Stapley, Bill Pearson, James Lindsay, Keith Morgan, Bill Davis, Kevin Gaul, John Stewart, Martin Haynes and the legendary John Ryle. We laughed together, we cried together and we stood together.

I owe a debt of gratitude to all my clients and their teams, especially those I have worked with over the past decade, during which we have explored, developed, tested and proven much of the content in this book. I would particularly like to thank Lyn Rees for his kind words in the foreword of this book, as well as Ingmar Elm, Achim Cremer and Mark Ashton at MAD for their perspectives and good humour when exploring some of the ideas and concepts contained in the book. I also thank a small team of volunteer reviewers: Jo Cross, Andie Hallihan and Mike O'Dell. I shall forever be in your debt.

I also acknowledge Alfred Brendel's playing of Beethoven's complete collection of piano sonatas, which makes the perfect accompaniment to writing.

Last but not least, I would like to thank the team at Inspired By Publishing, in particular Angela Haynes-Ranger, who has worked tirelessly to help me express myself more clearly in written form. I have learned much; I have much still to learn.

Thank you all.

Dedication

This book would not have been possible without the unflinching support, dedication and unwavering belief of my talented wife, Sarah. I love you.

Our family – and our beloved best friends Eric, Percy and Lady Gaga – are the glue in our relationship. While we welcome Lulu to the team, Sarah and I shall forever miss our dearly beloved Zeppelin.

This book is dedicated to the glue in your life that turns chaos into connection and binds purpose, people and passion, which you don't notice until it's gone.

Foreword

In the world of business, there are a few constants. Markets shift. Technology evolves. Strategies pivot. But one truth endures: The quality of a senior leadership team (SLT) is often the defining factor in whether an organisation merely survives or truly thrives. In *Lighting the Blue Touch Paper*, Les Murray brings four decades of unparalleled experience to bear on this exact challenge, offering not just a roadmap for building strong leadership teams but a compass for leading with purpose, integrity and impact.

Les Murray is not just an author. He is, in every sense of the word, a guide. Over the course of his 40-year career, Les has worked with over 100 senior leadership teams across industries, continents and cultures. He has seen the inner workings of organisations at their best and at their most fractured. Through it all, his insight, presence and unwavering commitment to truth and performance have helped unlock transformation where it matters most: at the very top.

To say Les is "experienced" is to understate his contribution to leadership development. He is a world-class executive coach, a trusted advisor to CEOs and a master facilitator of high-impact leadership events that shift not just strategies, but mindsets. What sets Les apart is not just his understanding of leadership theory or his familiarity with team dynamics; it is his ability to translate that understanding into meaningful change. He doesn't offer abstract frameworks or academic concepts. He offers hard-won, road-tested wisdom earned from thousands of hours in the room with some of the most senior, successful and occasionally stuck leadership teams on the planet.

This book is a distillation of that wisdom.

At its core, *Lighting the Blue Touch Paper* is about performance. Real, sustained, human performance. Les understands that SLTs are not just collections of smart, talented individuals. They are complex ecosystems of ambition, ego, vision, insecurity, resilience and aspiration. When they are aligned, they can move mountains. When they are misaligned, they can paralyse entire organisations. Les's gift lies in helping teams navigate that complexity with clarity and courage.

What makes this book so powerful is how grounded it is in reality. Les doesn't romanticise the work of leadership. He acknowledges how hard it is, how demanding, how frustrating and how often it is thankless. However, he also shows how deeply rewarding it can be when done right. He understands the pressures that SLTs face: the relentless pace, competing priorities and the need to deliver results while also building culture, strategy, trust and talent. He's been in those conversations. He's facilitated those off-sites. He's asked the tough questions that leaders avoid and then stood beside them as they answered with honesty.

Every chapter in this book is laced with practical tools, real-world examples and deeply human insights. You'll find guidance on everything from establishing shared purpose to managing interpersonal dynamics to building a cadence of performance and accountability. But more than that, you'll feel Les's presence on every page. His calm clarity, his quiet strength and his belief that great leadership is not just possible, but necessary.

One of the defining features of Les's work is his ability to hold both the system and the soul. He sees the broader organisational structures and strategy that shape leadership, but he never loses sight of the people inside them. He works at the intersection of personal growth and business impact, helping leaders sharpen their effectiveness by bringing more of their humanity to the table. This balance of heart and head, of ambition and humility, is what elevates his work above the rest.

If you are a CEO, a senior leader or someone tasked with developing leadership at the highest levels, this book is your essential companion. It doesn't offer shortcuts or simple answers because leadership isn't simple. What it offers instead is perspective. And that, as anyone who has worked with Les will tell you, is his superpower.

Les sees what others miss. He names the elephants in the room with kindness and courage. He helps teams see themselves more clearly, not through judgment, but through curiosity. And he holds a mirror up to leaders with the kind of grace that allows them to step into their next level, not defensively, but with intention and purpose.

I've seen firsthand the impact Les has on teams. I've watched leaders move from polite dysfunction to courageous collaboration. I've seen strategy sessions turn from sterile slide decks into galvanising calls to action. I've seen teams leave his sessions not just with action plans, but with a deeper sense of shared identity and renewed commitment. This book captures that magic and offers it to anyone ready to take the work seriously.

Ultimately, *Lighting the Blue Touch Paper* is not just about teams. It's about what happens when people decide to lead together, intentionally, courageously and in service of something larger than themselves. It's about what happens when leaders stop competing with one another and start co-creating a future that none of them could shape alone. Les doesn't promise that this is easy. But he does promise that it's worth it.

In an era when leadership is more crucial and more tested than ever, this book arrives as both a resource and a challenge. A resource for those who want to do the work well. A challenge for those willing to look beyond titles and roles and into the real work of building trust, alignment and shared accountability at the top.

Les Murray has spent a lifetime in the room where it happens, quietly shaping the conversations that shape organisations. In this book, he brings you into that room. Read it carefully. Read it generously. And most of all, use it. Because the strength of your senior leadership team will define the strength of your organisation – and there is no better guide to that journey than Les Murray.

Lyn Rees
Group Chief Executive, Novacyt Plc
April 2025

Preface

"The strength of the team is each individual member.
The strength of each member is the team."
– Phil Jackson, Basketball Coach

Before setting out to write this book, I asked myself the question: "Does the world need yet another business book?"

Obviously, I thought the answer was "yes."

In my mind, what the world does not need is another book crammed full of research and theories about human motivation in the workplace, nor endless well-crafted case studies of companies that subsequently fall from grace. To be clear, this is not a book about executive leadership; it is a book about executive teamwork and, in particular, the key factors of success that propel senior leadership teams.

I was inspired to write this book on igniting the energy, clarity and performance of senior leadership teams (SLTs) through a combination of lived experience, reflection and the privilege of learning alongside others. Over the years, I have experienced "the good, the bad and the downright ugly" of SLTs and how they can energise or drain an organisation. My own journey has been shaped not only by personal involvement in leadership and direct participation in several SLTs, but also by deep reading, private study and a relentless curiosity about what makes senior teams thrive or falter. The most inspiring aspect has been the opportunity to work closely with a diverse range of businesses, both in the UK and internationally, each offering a unique perspective on how strategy, culture and team dynamics are applied in practice. This book is my attempt to distil those insights into something practical, reflective and above all, useful to those who lead at the top and who face the challenges of growing and scaling businesses.

The final push to write this book comes from an anecdote I stumbled upon by chance, about Charles Handy, the maverick management guru who spent 100 days a year earning, 100 days a year writing and 100 days having fun, and devoted the rest to volunteering. Charles Handy observed that there are three occupations for which no qualification or training exists: politician, parent and manager. "Unfortunately, they were three of the most important," he observed. "Management, especially, was something almost everyone thought they could master. Rather like making love, it was something that sensible people instinctively knew how to do, when and as the need arose."[1] And so it is with teamwork.

The challenge with teamwork is that we all make numerous assumptions about what needs to be done, by whom, when and in what order. We rarely stop to consider how our own behaviour contributes to and negates what we, and others, are trying to achieve. And we seldom, if ever, think we are just plain wrong in our shattered expectations.

We don't so much need a book as we do active engagement. This book is written as that spark that lights up awareness, prompts questions and encourages exploration. It is written from the perspective of somebody who has been contracted time and again to produce a strategy, grow sales, cut costs, simplify operations and, on all occasions, "make it happen." In my honest endeavours to meet the expectations of a client and a manager, the people piece is rarely mentioned at the outset. It is assumed. It is taken for granted that I will come up with an answer that will become common sense and be ready for adoption. The reality, of course, is that I spend more time working out what is acceptable, what success really looks like and what it takes, as well as who needs to be on board to drive it through. Technical solutions, however elegant their design, are always secondary to the whims of people who carry an emotional intransigence to change.

Teamwork is understood, but it is practised unevenly.[2] The "knowing-doing gap" in respect of teamwork is a triumph of haste over consideration, assumption over knowledge and fear over love. Teamwork is frequently touted as a panacea for what needs to happen around here to improve, much like chanting "getting closer to the customer" is not a strategy when it lacks a specific action plan. Much like strategy, teamwork is not effective as a slogan, and its application does not come easily. The complexity is born by the very ingredient that gives rise to it – people – and the fact that we are products of an evolutionary process where we are all wired to react rather than consider how we respond.

There may be a few concepts which are new introductions to the reader of this book. However, much of the material here is likely familiar. After all, it is a topic where we can all lay claim to experience, and those of us not blessed with doubt may consider ourselves experts. Often, it is those experts who fail to connect with others, require more time and effort beyond what is considered natural, and quickly judge and condemn. This book is not for an expert fuelled by the latest management theory. Nor is this book for the follower of the school of thinking which emphasises optimising an individual's authority and command.

One of the unforeseen and unintended consequences of much current teaching is that it encourages people to ensure their voice is heard more, how to influence others more and an overall unhealthy obsession with individual impact. Such teaching is counterproductive to effective teamwork. If nothing else, this book encourages the reader to view the world through the "team lens" and challenge oneself to ask, "What can I do, or contribute, that will help others on the team progress and achieve more?"

There is ample evidence that shows a team will outperform and outlast any individual if and only if the contributors can come together and ensure that the whole is greater than the sum of its individual parts. To do so requires a higher level of self-awareness of oneself and others than is frequently assumed to generate the necessary foundational alignment for achieving desired outcomes.

This book is organised into three themed sections: Create (Chapters 1 to 4), Build (Chapters 5 to 7) and Sustain (Chapters 8 to 10). Although you may find yourself juggling elements of all three phases simultaneously, the book is designed to be read in sequence. Working through the book chapter by chapter provides an opportunity to reflect on your own team's journey as it unfolds.

At the end of each chapter, a brief set of reflective questions is provided to encourage deeper thinking. These are intended to help you apply the ideas shared here in practice and may encourage you to revisit earlier sections with fresh insight. At the end of the book, a fuller series of questions related to each chapter is provided for review. Whether you work through them alone or with your team, they are designed to prompt you to take stock and reflect on the progress made, the challenges faced and what specific action steps now need to be taken. Used in this way, the book functions more like a workbook, supporting you in bridging the gap between knowing and doing, and helps you resist the pull of quick fixes, lazy habits or surface-level change.

We all reap what we sow. As the stories herein will illustrate, senior teams are fragile creations. A sudden drop in energy or an abrupt loss of clarity is all it takes to poison the well. Senior teams require constant attention, and as my late mother-in-law was fond of saying, "A plant does not grow any faster by pulling on it."

Coming together is the first step. It is through shared effort, trust and collaboration that real success takes shape. No matter the challenge, it's the power of teamwork that turns potential into progress and ambition into achievement.

All the best,
Les Murray
www.20-20management.com

Contents

Introduction

"Theories are like toothbrushes. Everyone has one, and no one wants to use anyone else's."
– Anonymous

This Introduction sets out a compelling case for investing in the development of senior leadership teams (SLTs) as the single greatest lever for improving organisational performance, culture and long-term growth. It describes the immense influence SLTs have over strategic direction, resource allocation and enterprise-wide alignment, and why simply assembling talented individuals is not enough.

At its core, the summary introduces a practical blueprint for building and sustaining a high-performing SLT. The blueprint is drawn from decades of experience, cross-sector leadership insights and global best practices. It details the six critical dynamics that drive performance at the top: clarifying shared goals, defining distinctive roles, establishing behavioural norms, as well as execution, innovation and continuous renewal.

Whether you're scaling a business, navigating transformation or building capability, the blueprint provides a clear framework for turning leadership potential into sustained enterprise impact.

The Room at the Top

The senior team possesses extraordinary power and influence in a business. SLTs are the primary architects of the business strategy, which shapes the future direction by specifying the business vision and mission of the organisation. SLTs define how the organisation's purpose is to be delivered, determining the current and future market position and the related value proposition, as well as making decisions that allocate the most valuable available resources of capital, talent and time. That the SLT is the principal force in aligning the company's efforts towards a common goal cannot be overstated.[1] By setting clear priorities, aligning teams around shared objectives and ensuring accountability, the SLT moves an entire company toward its vision.

A SLT's competence and calibre significantly impact a company's trajectory. The SLT is the strategic decision-making body that makes informed choices, determining a company's ability to weather storms, adapt to disruptions and recover from setbacks. SLTs may choose to drive and shape mergers, acquisitions and company restructuring initiatives that transform operations. These BIG decisions can redefine market positioning, expand market reach and create new competitive advantages. The ability to face into and lead in high-pressure situations amplifies the SLT's influence and underscores its power over a company.

The SLT's disposition, behaviour and the language it employs ensure that it is the single most important influencer of an organisation's culture. Through their actions, SLT leaders set the tone for how employees interact, the kind of work environment they create and what activities and behaviours are valued within the organisation, such as collaboration, innovation and performance. SLTs have a profound impact on talent acquisition, development and retention strategies. Their decisions shape organisation structures and the resulting patterns of work as well as the development of management and staff at all levels. By identifying and nurturing high-potential talent, senior leaders can ensure a company's long-term success by building a capable and motivated workforce.

The SLT represents the public face of a company to investors, regulators, customers, suppliers and partners. Leaders with strong networks and credibility in their sector and markets can open doors, secure key partnerships and negotiate favourable deals at speed.

The scope and influence of an SLT on company performance are not up for debate. The SLT sets the ambition, pace and tone of a company.[2] When leaders align, everything accelerates. When SLTs are misaligned, confusion spreads, momentum stalls and even the best strategies fall flat. SLTs hold extraordinary power and influence, as their decisions impact every aspect of a company's performance, culture and long-term sustainability. Through their strategic authority, resource control and influence on the external and internal environments, the leadership team holds the keys to driving success.[3]

Home Truths

Effective SLTs do not just happen by bringing some talented people together and handing them the keys to the executive suite. It takes time, energy and commitment to create and build an effective team, and even more in a team invested with the responsibility of leading others.[4]

Leadership Commitment

A prerequisite of membership in an SLT is "all in" commitment. Everyone is sworn in, moving in lockstep, to achieve shared goals. Without "all in" commitment, groups perform as individuals; with it, they become a powerful unit of collective performance. "All in" commitment demands a shared purpose in which team members passionately believe, so that they can grow themselves and others and deliver. Without such a drive being evident, SLTs will fail to ignite, inspire and lead others to perform at a higher level.

Leading a Business, Not a Function

Leading a business requires a shift from functional excellence to enterprise leadership, where success is measured not just by what you deliver, but also by how well you empower others and drive the entire system forward. To be effective, senior leaders must understand their specific roles and accountabilities, as well as how they fit into the overall structure of the organisation and contribute to the business. As such, a condition of being part of a high-performing SLT is cheering on others who excel in complementary areas beyond one's own natural skill base, as well as being cheered on by peers.

In a healthy SLT, the members recognise the SLT as their "first team" and not the function/department that they lead. In addition, the achievement of business goals becomes the focus of a function/department's goals and not vice versa.

Team Players

The most effective way to improve business performance is to develop or replace senior team leaders. In high-performing teams, individuals come to understand the importance of focusing on elevating team performance before considering their own individual contributions. In high-performing leadership teams, there is little or no space for ego and the cult of the individual. Mavericks, however "brilliant" they may be, invariably become disruptive "lone wolves" and a source of friction.

Team players who model and reward vulnerability go on to create a more open, trusting and collaborative workplace that stimulates greater innovation, productivity and talent retention than any one individual is capable of.[5] As such, the SLT needs to demonstrate the behaviours, work ethic and values expected from others. No exceptions, no favourites, no backsliding.

Leaders Develop Leaders

Exceptional SLTs naturally develop leadership talent in their people to create an "upward draught" of talent who are ambitious and want to achieve more. This is done by promoting:

- Authenticity and transparency vs politicking

- Engagement and dialogue vs a "command and control" operating model

- Coaching vs directing by leading with questions[6]

- Promoting standards of excellence vs mediocrity

In the workplace, a vast untapped human potential is lost as a result of treating people as subordinates and devaluing their importance. People who accept taking orders usually run at half speed, under-utilising their potential initiative. They only ever do what they have been asked for and "watch the clock." Exceptional SLTs build organisations that foster connection, trust, collaboration, self-confidence, caring, commitment and consistent, clear communication. In doing so, they encourage people to innovate, play, have fun and deliver outstanding results built on above-average levels of emotional intelligence rather than relying solely on IQ per se.

The SLT Blueprint

The SLT blueprint serves as a guide to the key dynamics present in a high-performance senior team, combining strategic skills and insights required to drive and grow a business.

The inspiration for the leadership blueprint comes from many sources. First among these are the multiple articles, interviews, research studies and white papers published by business schools such as Harvard, Wharton, Princeton and Stanford, as well as more Anglo-centric teachings shared by institutions like Cranfield, London Business School, Warwick, INSEAD, IESE and IMD.

Many influential thinkers and teachers have written and shared material on leadership and strategy down the generations, including Brene Brown, Jim Collins, Peter Drucker, James Kouzes and Barry Posner, Patrick Lencioni, David Marquet, Roger Martin, John Maxwell, Michael Porter and Simon Sine, as well as well-conducted research studies, including Google's Project Aristotle.

Lastly, there is the lived experience of applying strategic restructuring, leadership development and business growth skills, having worked with the leadership teams of more than 100 FTSE 250 clients and high-growth "scale-ups" for over 40 years.

Distilling the key ingredients of this life's work, the SLT blueprint to achieve business growth comprises six interrelated elements:

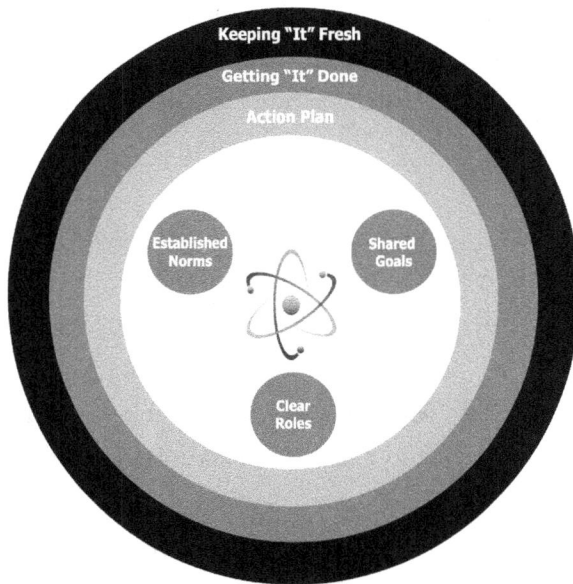

1. Shared Goals

Purpose-driven leadership. The SLT must define and communicate a clear, compelling vision that emphasises not just financial success but goes beyond commercial objectives to express a wider social and community purpose. This higher purpose resonates across the entire organisation. It is expressed in a form that inspires employees, customers and stakeholders and does not claim to be something the business is plainly not.

Strategic thinking. Leaders focus on the long-term – not just short-term profits. This includes building business models and strategies that focus on innovation and that anticipate future market shifts. Business strategy is the product of rigorous thinking, which avoids sleepwalking into activities that follow the competition, devalue product and service offerings, or shortchange employees. The quality of thinking determines the quality of business, so it is vital that senior team leaders can both challenge and be challenged in determining the way forward.[7]

Values. The senior leadership team seek to balance the needs of all stakeholders: employees, customers, suppliers, investors and the community. SLTs define the business goals and demonstrate the responsibility that flows from them, reflecting the organisation's core values in every decision. Otherwise, goals will never become shared, nor will they stand a chance of meaningful interpretation and implementation.

2. Clear Roles

Organisation design and structure. The organisation created serves to realise the business goals and strategy that have been created. At its simplest, SLTs lead teams of people who are resourced and deployed on business processes which are designed to deliver outcomes to customers. In short, the number of leaders around the top table of any organisation is a function of the complexity of the company's value proposition, bandwidth and competencies required to assure performance.

Leaders have defined accountabilities for the organisational units, comprising the distinctive capabilities and skills that coexist within the organisational structure they lead, regardless of the organisational form it adopts, as well as accountability to their peers who depend on their colleagues to deliver. Therefore, it follows that leaders must "champion their own" by ensuring the voice of their organisation's unit (e.g. function or department) is heard when making the most critical decisions that determine the future direction, investment and resource allocation. However, they must also encourage cross-functional teamwork that leverages diverse perspectives and skill sets to drive meaningful action. SLT leaders will find themselves constantly challenged in navigating the balance between long-term and short-term objectives.

Empowerment and accountability. Leaders must create an environment where staff at all levels are empowered with the appropriate delegated authority to make decisions that align with the company's goals. Accountability structures and mechanisms must be established to ensure that key performance metrics are met.

Provoke and channel constructive conflict. The reality of growth businesses is that organisational units, typically in the form of functions and departments, often conflict over the "right way to act" in any given situation. Rather than responding to such conflict in a way which seeks to minimise or downplay what is often at stake, conflict should be encouraged to flesh out the fundamental thinking blocks that constitute the rationale behind the "right way to act." Without the actively engaged debate over "the right way to act," whatever is decided upon will lack commitment, and the organisation will suffer the consequences. Once the "right way to act" is established, it is the duty of SLT leaders to channel the energy expended in conflict into collaboration to achieve success.

3. Established Norms

Embrace the "soft stuff." Leaders should be respectful, considerate and, above all, kind. One would think that would be a given, but it's rarely observed. More often, leaders are performance-focused, metric-oriented and hard taskmasters. Kindness in leadership fosters trust, collaboration and loyalty, creating a positive environment where people feel valued and motivated to contribute their best.

The reality is the soft stuff *is* the hard stuff. It takes guts and much courage to listen with an open heart and mind to anything and everything that comes your way. The best thing is to "press pause" and accept that criticism makes you strong. It is a triumph of the human spirit to embrace it, savour it and respond to it with the care, love and attention of its source.[8] If you want to stay well-informed, do not shoot the messenger. Collaboration is not fluffy; it involves a lot of back-and-forth, debate and listening to understand. Certainly, the most effective collaborators in business are team members who become great leaders when they learn to shift their focus from themselves to others.

Analytics and insight. Senior leadership teams, in all their forms, aim to harness data analytics to track progress and inform decision-making. Exceptional teams go further by using data not only to identify inefficiencies and spark innovation, but also to anticipate shifts in regulation, customer preferences or environmental conditions that require proactive strategic adjustments. But as strategies evolve, so too must the metrics by which success is measured. Aligning KPIs with the direction of travel ensures focus, relevance and impact. In this context, verifiable evidence should be a non-negotiable touchstone for discussion. Fact-checking is not "bureaucracy gone mad," it's a competitive advantage.

Focus on quality outcomes. Establish clear, measurable goals and track performance against targets. Ensure regular performance reviews and "1-2-1s" are action-oriented and focused on "moving the needle" on the value-enhancing activity that makes the difference in the business. Do not tolerate fluff on what counts and create a culture where speaking the hard truths is respected, not reprimanded.

Develop, develop, develop. Be equally concerned with developing others as with producing business results. Strong leaders develop others, which presumes good intentions, so recruit and select wisely to accelerate return on investment. A business grows through developing a pipeline of leaders who share the company's values and are equipped to drive its long-term goals. Senior leaders should actively prioritise mentorship, training and leadership development programmes that align with the company's purpose. There are few more productive moments in business than making yourself redundant by appointing a smarter person than yourself to your role, whilst ensuring you move on to working on the next big thing.

Diversity and Inclusion. A diverse (different genders, ethnic backgrounds, ages, abilities and educational experiences) leadership team is more likely to promote and build innovative ideas that drive future revenues. By planning leadership transitions, companies can avoid relying on tribal group role models. There is ample evidence that shows diverse leadership teams are more innovative and adaptable as they are more inclined to share and explore different perspectives that creatively address challenges and then lead with agility.

4. Action Plan

Understanding the market and customers. Leaders should stay actively wired into customer needs and preferences. By engaging with customers and understanding market dynamics, leaders can more effectively guide their companies toward delivering high-value products and services in a way that builds loyalty and advocacy, maximising earned revenue.[9] The alternative is thinking in an ivory tower of "shoulds and coulds," which will never be.

The clarity of road maps. Senior leaders design, develop and regularly update progress on roadmaps, making action plans more effective and sharper. Leaders are intentional beings, and to demonstrate intention, a road map is a prerequisite for a function or department, as well as for setting a path for the entire business. The SLT works to ensure alignment between all the working parts of a roadmap, so that there is a clear line of sight from top to bottom on what is happening, why and what is happening next. The creation and communication of a single, enterprise-wide and fully aligned roadmap is foundational to securing engagement throughout a business.

5. Getting "It" Done

Vision and execution. Vision without execution is a hallucination, whilst execution without vision is a nightmare. Be sure there is a collective process (e.g. Objectives and Key Results (OKRs), north star metrics or Hoshin Kanri) that is understood by all. This should be supported by quality data that translates the vision for the "big idea" into doable, practical and actionable small steps that ordinary people, who were not part of the "big idea's" conception, can fulfil. Senior leaders play a fundamental role in coaching, nudging and inspiring action, ensuring accountability for results and capturing learning.

Close the knowing-doing gap. Develop a work culture that encourages taking action rather than endless debate, which promotes "analysis paralysis" and "sweating the small stuff." At its heart, business is very simple – endeavour to keep it that way. Take the time to think through the strategy and turn it into an actionable plan for implementation. Be sure to establish a management execution system (e.g. OKRs) that empowers others, enables and tracks strategy implementation. Emphasise that learning and doing go hand in hand, and reward experimentation and calculated risk-taking. Regular feedback on what works and what doesn't will promote ongoing and iterative improvement.

Innovation and scaling. Growing businesses must be adaptable and scalable to thrive. Leaders should encourage experimentation with new ideas and processes that can increase efficiency, reduce waste and enhance product offerings. Once tested and trialled, initiatives that demonstrate evidence of success can then be rolled out across the organisation.

6. Keeping "It" Fresh

Continuous learning and adaptability. Encourage a growth mindset where leadership teams are always learning, adapting and innovating.[10] The business environment is constantly evolving, and leaders must foster an agile mindset that can pivot to meet changing market conditions, regulations and consumer expectations. This demands a means for effective two-way communication that establishes a rhythm and cadence for the business, informing and unifying different teams across the organisation. Above all else, don't outsource thinking to AI tools; rather, use AI tools to stimulate fresh thinking.

Tracking and updating. A successful business recognises that its journey is ongoing. Leadership teams must regularly review their progress against established goals and adjust their strategies as needed. This requires establishing robust feedback loops in meetings, in all their many forms, and across communication channels to understand how well practices are working and where improvements are needed.

When Senior Leadership Teams Drift, Businesses Bleed

Most senior leadership teams (SLTs) look functional. Meetings happen, strategies are announced and results arrive (just about). But research tells us a different story:

- Only 8% of executives believe their senior team is truly effective (McKinsey).[11]

- 1 in 4 senior leaders can clearly articulate their key strategic priorities.[12]

- 65% of senior executives experience a clash between functional and enterprise accountabilities, highlighting a widespread lack of clarity about how the executive team's collective work really adds value across the business.[13]

- More than half of senior teams report persistent issues of misalignment, low trust and ineffective collaboration[14,15]

- Senior leaders waste 15% of collective time in unproductive meetings (Bain).[16]

- 72% of organisations make as many bad decisions as good ones (McKinsey).[17]

The costs of inaction are high and mostly hidden until it's too late.

Problem	Hidden Cost	Visible Consequence
Misalignment	Duplication, slow execution	Lost revenue and wasted investment in staff costs
Poor decisions	Bad calls equal good ones	Sunk costs and missed growth opportunities
Unproductive meetings	15% wasted time	£135k+ annual salary burn (assumes 6-person SLT only)

Problem	Hidden Cost	Visible Consequence
Low trust	Silence, risk aversion	Stalled innovation and loss of talent
Failure to cascade	65% of employees simply do not understand strategy	Disengagement and poor execution
Silos and politics	Turf wars, friction	Slow culture and lost agility

The reality is that SLT dysfunction is not neutral. Every day, it bleeds time, money, energy and talent from your business. Leaders who wait for the next resignation, distraction or crisis before acting simply make the eventual repair far more expensive. The smart move? Act *now*. Build the team the business deserves, and that the strategy requires, before all the hidden costs are seen in financial results.

Conclusion

A highly effective SLT has the power to shape the trajectory of an entire organisation. Its influence extends well beyond day-to-day operations: setting strategic direction, shaping culture and modelling the behaviours that cascade through every level of the business. The collective quality of leadership at the top and its ability to unify are often the most accurate predictors of long-term success.

The leadership blueprint for a growing business combines visionary thinking with practical execution while balancing innovation with resilience. SLT leaders must be strategic, adaptable, emotionally intelligent and committed to fostering a positive culture. Equally vital are distinctive roles that ensure every leader brings complementary strengths while avoiding duplication or confusion.

Highly effective teams establish clear norms for how they operate, communicate and hold each other accountable.[11] What sets exceptional leadership teams apart is their ability to delegate effectively and make data-informed decisions as they navigate the complexities of growth and scale, especially when under pressure. Execution is the acid test of any leadership. High-performing SLTs maintain a relentless focus on execution, supported by robust management systems that turn strategy into operational reality. Finally, high-performing senior teams do not stand still. They embed innovation as a team habit, continuously challenging assumptions, seizing opportunities and adapting to change.

Together, these elements create a senior leadership team that not only performs but also transforms. The objective measure of success lies in building a strong, cohesive SLT that leads the organisation to deliver on its promise while staying true to its core values as it grows.

A helpful metaphor to guide your thinking is that of a football team climbing the leagues. The squad that earns promotion from the lower divisions rarely makes it all the way to the Premier League unchanged. As the stakes rise, so do the demands: sharper skills, deeper expertise and fresh thinking and approaches become essential.

The team continues to evolve, adapting its line-up and style of play, but its core values, work ethic and shared ambition remain the foundation.

The challenge is to grow the team's reach and impact without losing what made it special in the first place. Great senior leadership teams don't just run businesses; they shape them. And in doing so, they are shaped by the future they commit to building.

Chapter 1
The Right Stuff

"When you see people with 'the right stuff,' those who choose the right over the wrong or the 'iffy,' let them know you're proud of them."
– Price Pritchett, Consultant

Finding the right people for senior leadership roles is one of the most consequential decisions any organisation can make. It's about more than ticking boxes for experience or technical skill; it's about recognising the mindset, behaviours and values that enable someone to thrive in a complex, fast-moving environment. This chapter examines the deeper qualities that define outstanding leadership candidates and the practical challenges of accurately and fairly assessing them in real-world settings.

Drawing on lived experiences, memorable anecdotes and sharp insights from leaders across sectors, this chapter challenges conventional recruitment norms. It introduces practical actions to create an ideal candidate profile, with concepts such as the "sower-grower-mower" model and the GWC review that help cut through noise and identify individuals who are not just a good fit on paper, but a genuine fit for the business and its stage of growth. These ideas highlight the importance of emotional intelligence, adaptability and enterprise thinking, which are attributes often overlooked in favour of polished credentials or "safe" choices.

Beyond selection, the chapter also addresses the critical importance of onboarding. It outlines how to accelerate trust, build team cohesion and create a psychologically safe environment where new leaders can truly contribute. The goal is not simply to fill a role, but to embed someone who elevates the team, aligns with the company's values and helps shape the culture and performance of the business for years to come.

The Ideal Candidate

In the very early days of my career, I had the honour and privilege of working closely with an inspirational business leader whose work ethic and engaging style left an indelible impression upon me. He regularly worked himself to exhaustion. On one notable occasion, he suddenly collapsed and fell into a deep sleep during a dinner whilst on a business trip in the USA. It was a character trait I recognised as unhealthy, but he earned everybody's respect as he was not somebody to burn the candle at both ends. He just worked hard, kept at it and did not appear to know when to stop. He inspired a work ethic that has served me well.

I recall that in one of our early meetings, I asked what it was he was looking for when he hired people. I unwittingly tapped into a vein of golden wisdom.

"When I meet candidates for the first time, I imagine they are wearing a giant zip that runs from their mouth down to their navel.

My task is to pull that zip as far down as I can and see what fire is burning in their belly. I want to see how fierce that fire is and what causes it to ignite. Once I come to know it, the zip goes back up and the meeting can really get rolling. All being well, they will enjoy meeting me, appreciate what I have to say and look forward to coming back next week to start work.

Then, once people are hired, I ensure they commit to truly immersing themselves in the business. They don't just clock in for a 9-to-5 day when they come through that door. They are expected to embrace what is in front of them, use their critical thinking skills and engage. I want them to feel that they can achieve so much more with what already exists: improve it, grow it, enhance it, expand it and accelerate it. They can only begin to do that if they have thrown themselves into really understanding what works, or, if not, by tracking it all back to root causes and developing a system-wide view.

Once they come back up for air and share their thinking, then the real work can start on how they can make their contribution and make a real difference. I shall be right there with them, cheering them on and giving whatever support I can muster to help them achieve more."

A strong, clear-headed view with much to be said in its favour. But, it is also one that was pregnant with unconscious bias and the risks of missing talent, because the candidate did not look the part or "fit in" as might be expected.

Fast forward 15 years, and I was participating as a regular panel member at a Professional Services firm's Assessment Centres to review and evaluate various job applicants and their fit with the business. The guiding mantra was simple: There is no such thing as a bad candidate, only a bad fit.

I shall always remember the occasion, one bright sunny spring day, when the panel assembled at a fine country house in the Home Counties to be briefed by a young HR manager who was championing a new 12-page evaluation form filled with multiple 1-10 scales and grids. The briefing lasted 15 minutes, and we were given 15 minutes to familiarise ourselves with the new form before the Assessment Day formally started.

"Absolute bollocks!" exclaimed the ageing grey guy with bushy eyebrows in the charcoal grey chalk pinstripe at the end of the Assessors' row of desks once the HR manager had left the room. "This is useless," he went on. "This is so bad. This stuff, well-intentioned as it is, and diligently produced, actually gets in the way of assessing today's candidates. This is so wrong!" In a firm that took pride in the progress yielded by its heavy investment in operating processes and systems, this was an extraordinary outburst from a senior partner.

"We all know they can read and write, add up and talk well. They would not be here if they couldn't. There are only three things that matter around here: Latin, Bunny and Pizzaz." Puzzled looks all around the room. He went on, "Let's not complicate the challenge. There are really only three qualities to assess."

Latin. Ask yourself: Can they think? Do they show the capacity to solve problems? Can they think from first principles and make do with the absence of data? Has the lift reached the top floor? Do they demonstrate a practical wisdom for how to get stuff done?

Bunny. Ask yourself: Do you actually like them? Do you feel yourself wanting to be with them? Could you share an 8-hour flight to Chicago sat next to them and enjoy their company? Do they make other people feel good just by being there?

Pizzaz. Ask yourself: Have they got flair? Do they exude style? Do they stand out from the grey and ordinary? Maybe have some chutzpah? Not brash, not brassy, but inspiring? Do they have the X factor? Do they bring sparkle? Are you moved by how they say it as much as by what they say?

"What we need to know is whether they are better than us, or whether they have the stuff to become so. To help figure that out, at the end of the day, we mark them as low, medium and high for each of Latin, Bunny and Pizzazz. The bar we set: a minimum of 2 highs and 1 medium. Anything less is not a fit with us."

All around the room, light bulbs switched on as one. We all instinctively pushed away the papers the HR manager had so earnestly distributed and talked excitedly about the day ahead, but they were too detailed, complex and not on point. We all knew why we were there, what to look for and how to engage as a group to make the decisions about "finding the right stuff" for the business.

As my early career days demonstrated, it is essential to understand what drives and motivates people and gain insight into the contributions they want to make and why. Understanding and wanting to support a person's purpose and energy for driving forward is fundamental. However, what really distinguishes a senior hiring decision is not the individual's knowledge, technical competence and ambition, but rather their "soft skills," such as communication, relationship building and presence. Crucially, it is the perspective formed on these "softer skills" that shapes the decision about "fit," closely followed by their ability to "hit the ground running" and add value, lead and deliver.

So, ask yourself: Do you have a clear vision and understanding of who you are hiring? Or do your processes and current cultural norms unwittingly lead you down a hazy, politically correct path that dumbs down decision-making into accepting averages and mediocrity?

Can you instinctively express the qualities of your ideal candidate without having to check a list of attributes that is filed away somewhere? Job descriptions help shape and define the role as well as give a recruiter a head start, but what about the person you are hiring? Can you precisely describe what you are looking for that will distinguish the ideal candidate? And if so, can you boil it down to just a few words which focus the mind?

Do you blindly accept what the recruitment process yields, namely, second best, rather than holding out for the candidate who will add to and strengthen the health of the organisation?

Hiring a senior leadership team is one of the most critical decisions the business leader can make, as these individuals will shape the strategy, culture and performance of the business.

Each leadership role requires specific skills and qualities that reflect a pedigree in a chosen field of functional excellence. However, the key theme of a preferred candidate, worldwide, is the ability to work effectively with others in the team. A highly effective Senior Leadership Team (SLT) must not only excel in their individual domains but also collaborate effectively to drive the business forward. Therefore, it follows that one must select individuals who complement each other's strengths and whose combined expertise can support the company in its various stages of future development and growth.

When evaluating candidates for an SLT, the ideal team player should embody a blend of strategic acumen, strong leadership presence, exceptional collaboration skills and a growth mindset to have an enterprise-wide impact.

Key Characteristics of the Right Stuff

Conversations with multiple MDs and CEOs have provided some invaluable insights into painful lessons learned about the ideal candidate's characteristics to hunt for. There is no single definitive list. However, there are key common attributes to sense check with your own worldview.

Strategic and Systems Thinking

- Can see the big picture and connect the dots between different business functions

- Demonstrates big picture thinking and foresight, and ensures strategies cascade

- Shows how to balance short and long-term goals by making clear trade-offs

Leadership Presence

- Possesses gravitas; conveys authority and stays calm under pressure

- Articulates vision, purpose and expectations in a compelling way

- Builds confidence through consistent words and actions

Decision-Making

- Comfortable making tough, high-stakes decisions in ambiguous circumstances and under pressure

- Balances analytical rigour with gut instinct

- Acts with confidence despite ambiguity

- Demonstrates accountability and takes ownership of both successes and failures

Emotional Intelligence (EQ)

- Self-aware and able to regulate emotions; knows how to adjust communication style to suit the audience effectively

- Shows empathy and actively listens to others' perspectives

- Reads and responds to others effectively

- Responds to criticism constructively

- Navigates conflicts diplomatically and builds strong relationships

Collaboration Skills

- Possesses a blend of low ego and high curiosity

- Listens to understand, not win

- Can influence others without relying on authority and job titles

- Can turn tension into effective and productive dialogue

- Communicates to bridge gaps between departments, regions and disciplines

Adaptability and Resilience

- Thrives on challenge and adapts well to changes in the environment

- May prefer a fast, dynamic pace, tuning into productivity rather than activity

- Learns from knock-backs and demonstrates perseverance

- Open to change, remains optimistic and tests and stretches current team thinking

Execution and Results Orientation

- Translates strategy into execution, ensuring ideas become actions

- Holds self and others accountable for delivering outcomes

- Stays focused on outcomes and seeks ways to improve performance and efficiency

Integrity and Values Alignment

- Demonstrates sound decision-making and trustworthiness

- Embodies and reinforces the company's mission, vision and values

- Stands by ethical decisions even when inconvenient

- Owns up to mistakes and leads with authenticity

Growth Mindset[1] and Learning Agility

- Stays curious

- Continuously seeks personal and professional development

- Learns from setbacks

- Actively seeks feedback and acts on it

- Challenges conventional thinking and encourages innovation and fresh approaches

Hiring

Hiring senior leaders is not an activity to rush into. Taking time to prepare the selection process that matches the profile of the role you are seeking to fill will pay off in the long term. While data and interviews are crucial, at the end of the day, you should trust your instincts. You'll be working closely with these people, so a sense of comfort and trust is important.

Experienced senior managers of large corporates can be utterly "lost at sea" in a young, dynamic scale-up. Likewise, an innovative freewheeling executive who has a track record of several growth journeys under his belt can simply "be lost" in a large corporate environment. Many high-growth SMEs lament hiring the "classy CV" that sparkles with qualifications and blue-chip brand experience. More often than not, such hires turn out to be flat, insipid and uninspiring encounters simply because there is an expectation and mindset mismatch between the role, the candidate and business dynamics.

Arguably, the most critical feature to be mindful of is hiring people who fit with the growth phase of the business and who are well-adapted to the pace of change the industry is experiencing.

You could begin by asking yourself: Do I need a sower, a grower or a mower for the role that I have in mind?[2] What is best suited for what the business needs?

The characteristics of each type can be simply expressed as:

Sower. Disrupter, entrepreneurial, change agitator. This person is not troubled by organisation charts and is already living in the desired future, and is frustrated by what exists today. Restless. Trailblazer. Direct and engaging. Driven by wealth creation and/or legacy. Winning doesn't just matter; it is everything. Emotions may bubble up to the surface. Frequently, the loudest and most eloquent voice in the room.

Grower. The living embodiment of a growth mindset, willing to move outside his comfort zone to focus on the art of the possible. Can do = will do. A low-maintenance self-starter who looks up and sees ahead. Confident. Capable. Phlegmatic. Gets stuff done. This person is motivated by achievement, enjoys mastering new skills and thrives on tackling general management challenges. Definitely not fazed by unknowns. A lifelong learner. Quickly moves onto the next thing.

Mower. Stable, low risk, safe pair of hands. Suspicious of change, so will only risk undertaking incremental change conservatively. Focuses on optimising how things happen. Thinks longevity and security. Tendency to seek out technically specialist roles. Polisher. Lives in the here and now. Sees things through to the end. Consistent. Disciplined. Determined. Resilient. Last person standing when everybody else has fallen.

The distinctions in the characteristics of a sower, grower and mower are much more about mindset and an individual's personal disposition and behaviour. Technical competence is neutralised.

The environment in which the contributions of each are optimised:

Sower: Start-up, business turnaround/transformation, high-change environment

Grower: People development, process/system introduction, execution orientation

Mower: Cash generation, optimisation

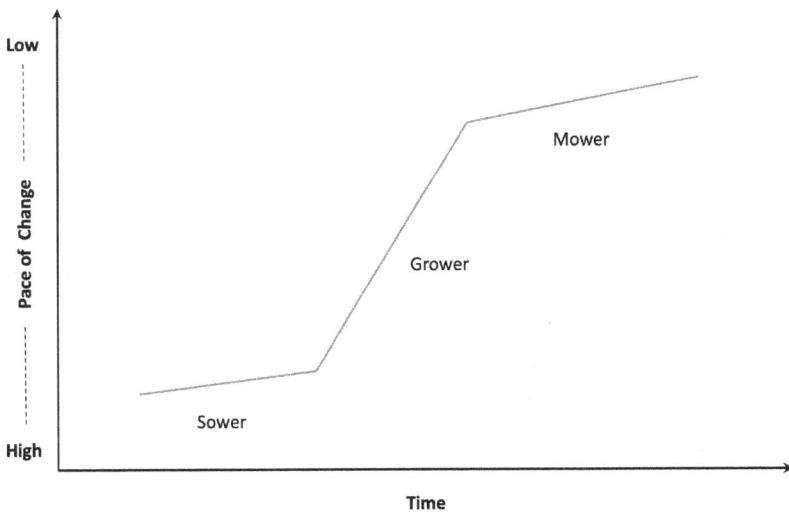

The key recruitment attributes for each include:

Sower: "trailblazer," "restless," "impact"

Grower: "shiny eyes," "corporate puzzle master," "1-2-3, get into action"

Mower: "steady," "calm," "methodical"

Once you have a clear picture of the ideal candidate's profile and their match with the business dynamics and pace of change, you reduce the risk of failure. This is especially true when the process is coupled with robust selection methods that blend behavioural interviews, panel discussions and case studies, together with psychometric and personality profiling, plus the all-important follow-through on references. When considering external candidates, I consistently advocate for telephone calls with at least two referees (career and/ or character) to invest quality time in really getting to know how an individual works. These calls can reveal a great deal of hidden value.

Every successful business establishes its own selection process and approach. But first and foremost, it is clear who it wants. I recall one hospitality client that had developed a small specialist function, led by a mature, PhD-qualified manager who could describe in exhaustive detail the precise required make-up of a successful candidate for operational management roles. He presided over an impressive data bank, and the rigour of the analyses went back several years. The business had developed a powerful predictor of performance based on data collected from thousands of individuals in various roles. The created data-led recruitment system was both impressive and accurate, and well ahead of its time. It was undoubtedly a source of competitive advantage to have such a decision support capability, enabling the matching of candidates to the various and diverse brands that demanded different degrees of emphasis on skills and aptitudes. However, it did not extend to the most senior levels of leadership.

There are very few businesses with data sets that can help predict the performance of a candidate for a senior leader's role with any accuracy.

Onboarding

Onboarding new SLT leaders requires more than just a functional introduction. It is about integrating them deeply into the team's dynamics, building trust quickly and fostering strong peer relationships. Lay the foundation for a smooth transition by clearly communicating expectations upfront. Most leading businesses will provide an onboarding pack that includes team bios, cultural values, key strategic priorities and organisational history, together with a summary of the most critical challenges.

I encourage clients to take onboarding senior colleagues to the next level by inviting existing SLT leaders to prepare a short personal video or letter introducing themselves, sharing their leadership philosophy and at least one vulnerability they have had to overcome during their leadership journey. This accelerates trust building and encourages newcomers to "drop the mask" and engage with their peers authentically and with courage. During the initial round of introductions, a peer buddy can be assigned to provide informal insights on team culture, unspoken norms and potential pitfalls.

The core objective when introducing new SLT leaders is to facilitate a smooth transition from surface-level interactions to establishing genuine, deep trust among peers. One way of doing this is to facilitate a private SLT meeting where each member shares:

- A brief life journey highlighting key personal and professional turning points

- Their "leadership scars," or the experiences that shaped their approach to leadership

- What excites them and what they fear most in their new role

Existing SLT leaders should be encouraged to reciprocate with similar sharing to establish common ground and bond in a way that helps to express and share behavioural norms. If recruitment forces clarity on defining roles, onboarding enables clarity on establishing norms.

In the days that follow, encourage structured 1-2-1s with each SLT leader where the conversation focuses on:

- "How do you like to work?"

- "What frustrates you in teams?"

- "What do you need from me to be successful?"

A typical leadership offsite would involve conducting vulnerability-based trust exercises inspired by Patrick Lencioni's *The Five Dysfunctions of a Team*, where each SLT leader shares a past failure and what they learned, as well as a "If you really knew me, you'd know that…" exercise.[3] This leads to a group commitment discussion that asks, "What are we willing to hold each other accountable for?" Finally, to enable the new leader to engage in a safe and structured debate with the team, conclude with a session on constructive conflict resolution, focusing on aligning shared decision-making norms and accountability expectations.

Match this activity with informal team get-togethers, such as lunches, "curry nights," or social events, to build personal relational capital before shifting the focus from individual integration to full team cohesion by hosting a leadership offsite with trust-building exercises.

As the onboarding phase closes, typically after 90 days, assign the new leader an early-impact project in collaboration with another SLT leader. It all helps to cement the bond of trust established with peers. You could also seek to involve the new SLT leader in a strategic decision to reinforce their position as a peer, not an outsider.

Onboarding should help recruits and existing SLT leaders progress through the four stages of psychological safety, where honesty is rewarded, past experiences and learnings are recognised and feedback becomes a part of everyday life, such that everyone feels comfortable challenging the status quo.

The 4 Key Success Factors of Onboarding New SLT Leaders

1. **Vulnerability from "The Top."** If the MD and senior leaders model openness, the new leader will likely follow suit.

2. **Structured, not just organic.** Intentional trust-building is essential; do not leave it to chance.

3. **Authenticity over formality.** Real bonding happens when people drop the corporate façade.

4. **Psychological safety.** Create a culture where leaders can express doubts and challenges without fear.

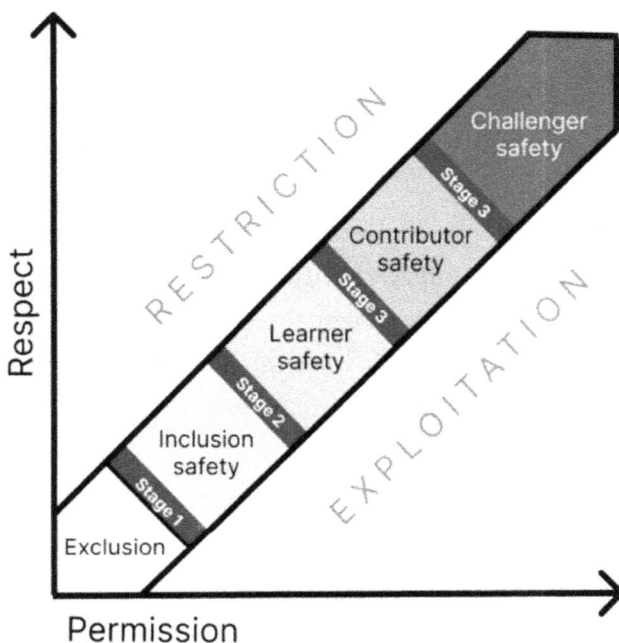

Source: Tim Clark, 4 Stages of Psychological Safety[4]

In her book, *The Fearless Organisation*, Amy Edmonson offers practical guidance for bringing psychological safety to life, but it can be distilled into three core behaviours.[5] They may sound simple, but remember, they need to extend into everything you do and communicate as a leader.

1. **Framework is a learning problem, not an execution problem.** The outcome of work is not the only output; it should also be a learning experience on how to do it better next time.

2. **Own the fact that you're human and therefore make mistakes.**
   Admit when you're wrong or (gasp!) don't know the answer. It
   will encourage others to do the same.

3. **Ask (a lot of) questions and be curious about everything.**
   When you ask your team about what they're doing or for their
   help, you're creating a space and a need for people to speak up
   – an essential part of psychological safety and high-performing
   teams.

It is an unfortunate truth that businesses invest significant amounts of
time and money in recruiting and hiring new staff, only to see many of
them leave within the first 12 months. The impact of high churn in an
SLT can cause a business to stall and lose momentum. Recruitment
costs money, and onboarding costs time. Each new leader brings with
them the potential to succeed and achieve more. To lose the passion
and energy that a new leader brings because of a lack of time invested
in onboarding is an opportunity lost.

Follow the advice of John Chambers (Chairman and former CEO of
Cisco Systems): "We focus first on the people and how we incorporate
them into our company, and then we focus on how to drive the
business."[6]

Making It Sticky

For an SLT to perform and ensure the business grows by making the
right decisions for the environment in which it operates, you need
to ensure that the right people are in the right seats doing the right
things. GWC, a tool first pioneered by Gino Wickman in *Traction*,

encourages leaders to quickly and objectively determine whether a business has the "right person in the right seat."[7] The tool simply requires one to ask three questions of your people:

1. Do they **G**et it?

2. Do they **W**ant it?

3. Do they have the **C**apacity to do it?

The answer to each is a non-negotiable "Yes" or "No." "Kind of" is not an option! When one answers these questions openly and honestly, and if any one of the three questions is a "no," then simply put that person is in the wrong seat. It's a very powerful exercise that can help highlight the real issues a company may be facing, and it is usually just one of three: communication, process or people. The common denominator to all three is, of course, people.

"Do they Get it?" is about a person having a deep, meaningful understanding of the role they have been hired for. When someone gets it, they have that intuitive feel, the natural aptitude for understanding what is required to deliver. A "no" simply means that this position isn't suitable for them and the company to get what it wants, and it's time to find someone else for this role.

"Do they Want it?" is about whether the work positively motivates them on a daily basis. Can they bring their whole self to the game every day, consistently, with enough energy to move them and the company forward at the required pace? If this work isn't what they truly want to do, they may find a way to do other things.

The "Capacity to do it" is fourfold. Do they have the mental, emotional, physical and time capacity to do the job – and do it well? For this, mental capacity relates to their abilities and knowledge. Emotional capacity is their understanding of how "what they do" impacts others. Physical capacity is related to the amount of endurance and dexterity required for the role. And finally, time capacity is tied to the number of days, hours, minutes and seconds success in the role will take.

SLT Member	Get it?	Want it?	Capacity?	Action
CEO				
CFO				
COO				
CSO				
CMO				
...				

It is for the individual to demonstrate they "get it" and "want it." They are the ones responsible for doing so. Of the three GWC questions, it is capacity that can be most developed, if the business is prepared to invest the effort in doing so to turn the role holder from "good to great."

The MD completes a GWC every 6 months alongside a company-wide talent management review of each individual's performance and potential to ensure that the right people are in the right role doing the right things right. I can think of several clients where completing such a review objectively can allow a remarkable amount of noise and friction to fade away by taking more deliberate steps, starting conversations that identify barriers to performance and developing action plans to overcome challenges. In some cases, it leads to parting company with people. More often than not, it results in a short coaching programme where hidden potential is unlocked by changing mindsets, perspectives and conversations that challenge "bad habits," comfort zones and a creeping acceptance of mediocrity.

Regular SLT GWC reviews support the foundations of a performance culture. This culture is comprised of vibrant and passionate role holders who are determined to play at the top of their game, positively motivated to make their mark in the universe, and are inspired by the people ahead of them to create an "upward draught" of talent pushing to excel and do more.

Summary

Creating a full profile of the ideal job candidate for an SLT role is a powerful investment in long-term performance. Beyond technical capability and career history, the most effective profiles capture mindset, values and outlook on risk, which are key factors in leadership decision-making, especially under pressure. An ideal SLT leader not only brings domain expertise but also aligns with the organisation's strategic ambitions, embraces accountability and is willing to challenge and be challenged in the service of shared goals. Their risk appetite, whether cautious or bold, must complement their role as well as the SLT's overall balance to ensure resilience, agility and growth.

Once appointed, the onboarding process plays a crucial role in helping a new leader feel a sense of psychological safety and a sense of belonging. Early alignment with team norms, clarity of role and access to informal and formal networks help embed confidence and trust. To sustain momentum, regular GWC (Get it, Want it, Capacity to develop) reviews, led by the MD, ensure that the individual continues to understand the role, remains motivated by it and is growing in their ability to deliver it at a high level. This creates a dynamic and self-aware leadership team, one that is better equipped to evolve with the business.

Reflective Questions

The questions set out below are designed to help you internalise key ideas, examine your own experiences in light of what you've read and consider how any insights might shape your thinking and actions in future. There are no right answers, only honest ones. Use these opportunities to reflect to deepen your awareness, spark conversation with others or simply increase awareness of what's changing for you as you make progress through this book.

Can you crisply express the ideal candidate for the SLT role that needs to be filled in a few words?

How will this new leader help drive your vision forward over the next 2 to 3 years?

What does the current SLT gain, or risk, by adding this person?

What behaviours and values are non-negotiable for someone joining your SLT?

Where will you need to adapt your own leadership to make space for them to succeed?

There is a longer list of questions in the "Appendix: Reflective Questions." These are designed to be addressed when you, with or without the team, have more time available for reflection, rather than reaction.

Chapter 2
Foundational Alignment

"Just as your car runs more smoothly and requires less energy to go faster and further when the wheels are in perfect alignment, you perform better when your thoughts, feelings, emotions, goals and values are in balance."
– Brian Tracy, Coach

Alignment is not about rigid agreement; it's about clarity, connection and shared direction. This chapter examines the fundamental building blocks that foster cohesion within a senior leadership team (SLT), arguing that foundational alignment is what distinguishes teams that deliver results from those that fail to do so. Misalignment, often subtle and unspoken, can quietly undermine trust, delay decisions and dilute execution, especially in high-stakes environments where speed, clarity and unity matter most.

Drawing on vivid real-world examples, including the costly missteps of global enterprises, this chapter highlights how assumptions, unclear roles and siloed thinking erode performance. It shows how high-performing SLTs invest time in strengthening connections, surfacing values, defining roles and aligning around shared goals. Rather than being an abstract exercise, alignment is presented as a daily practice that sits at the core of effective leadership, shaping behaviour, communication and ultimately, results.

What follows is a practical guide to building alignment that lasts. From trust-building exercises and role clarity tools to the development of shared values and the creation of a living SLT Charter, this chapter provides a template for creating a leadership team that thinks and acts as one. When foundational alignment is in place, momentum builds, collaboration deepens and the entire organisation gains clarity and confidence in the path ahead.

A Case Study of the Airbus A380: The Importance of Clarity

An SLT does not fail because of one big mistake. It fails because of small misalignments that go unaddressed. The misalignments are a function of a lack of shared clarity. Clarity on business goals, individual roles and company values and behaviours is the fuel that drives high-performance teams. All too often, clarity is taken for granted. Or worse still, it is assumed when, in fact, what exists is open to interpretation. Clarity in a team setting means that every member has a shared and unambiguous understanding of the goals, expectations, roles and the path forward. Clarity eliminates confusion, misalignment and wasted effort.

One of the most famous case studies of a team failing due to misalignment and incorrect assumptions is the development of the Airbus A380, the world's largest passenger plane. What was meant to be a triumph of engineering and global collaboration turned into a costly lesson in the importance of clear communication, alignment and assumption-checking.

What Happened?

In the early 2000s, Airbus set out to build the A380, a double-decker, wide-body jet designed to challenge Boeing. The project involved teams across multiple countries, with engineers in Germany, France, Spain and the UK working together.

Despite Airbus's history of successful collaborations, a single assumption about software compatibility led to a disaster.

The Wrong Assumption

The German and Spanish teams were using an older version of CATIA (software used for designing aircraft wiring), while the French and British teams used a newer version. The German and Spanish teams assumed that their designs would be compatible with the software used by the French and British teams. Meanwhile, the French and British teams assumed that the others would upgrade to the newer system. No one raised the issue until way too late in the process.

The Consequences

There were massive wiring errors. When Airbus tried to assemble the aircraft, the wiring systems did not fit together – literally. Over 500km of wiring had to be ripped out and redesigned, delaying the project by two years.

Additionally, there was financial fallout. The delays cost Airbus over €6 billion ($7.5 billion at the time), and Airbus' stock plummeted by

26% in a single day. Airlines waiting for the A380 had to reconsider their fleet plans, impacting customer confidence.

Lastly, the internal chaos. The blame game started between Airbus' divisions, damaging internal trust. Leadership had to step in and restructure project management across countries.

Key Lessons Learned

Never assume alignment. Just because teams are working on the same project in the same organisation does not mean they are on the same page.

Check for hidden misalignment early. If Airbus had tested compatibility earlier, it would have discovered the problem before it cost them billions. Regular cross-team alignment meetings and assumption checks could have prevented this.

Communication is key. The project failed not because of bad engineering, but because teams failed to communicate effectively. Thus, a system-wide approach to collaboration is critical.

The A380 was eventually completed and became a marvel of aviation, but the lack of demand from airlines and the severe financial losses led Airbus to stop production in 2021, just 14 years after it began. Assumptions, even small ones, can sink massive projects. If a company with the long-established credentials of international collaboration, such as Airbus, can make this mistake, any team can.

With the benefit of hindsight, such errors read like "schoolboy errors." Directors and managers often assume they are all on the same page when, in fact, they are not. How many times do you hear about product teams, marketing teams and engineering teams holding different views on what development to invest?

All too often, fiercely contested different points of view delay key decisions. Add a creeping culture of fear where "bad news" is filtered out before it reaches the top table, and SLT has unwittingly created a toxic cocktail unless the misalignment across functions is resolved. Experience has shown time and again that the reason teams fall apart and fail, especially when "things go sideways," is because the foundations of what builds a high-performing team have not been put in place. Rather, the rush to do the work we are here to do – "get ahead of the curve" and deliver results – is the very thing that gets in the way of a senior team succeeding.

For the avoidance of doubt, and to challenge any silent assumptions, practise the best test for clarity, which is to simply ask for confirmation that it exists and that each person can demonstrate a genuine understanding of it. When a decision is made, especially major ones, it pays to ask each team member to confirm their understanding of the key points: what has been agreed upon, the objectives, immediate next steps, execution and how it is best achieved.

Connection

Unless there is a working level of trust between all the members of the SLT, many initiatives will stall or not progress, as individuals will not be motivated to be proactive and look out for each other, offer advice or intervene if they see something going awry. The fact is, they will just let it happen and join the "blame fest" when it does. Trust needs to be earned and continually developed.

When building trust within a senior leadership team, it's important to invest in activities that foster vulnerability, deepen understanding and strengthen interpersonal connections. Here are ten of the best trust-building exercises that I have experienced that build connection at a deeper level between SLT leaders:

1. Personal Storytelling: Life's Defining Moments

Each team member shares key personal and professional experiences that shaped them. The exercise helps humanise colleagues, fosters empathy and encourages deeper connections. It works especially well in retreat settings with a relaxed atmosphere.

2. Trust Battery Check: Inspired by Shopify's Model

Each team member rates their trust level with colleagues on a scale of 1 to 100 and shares the reasons behind their rating. When working with someone new, the trust battery typically starts at 50%. The exercise helps identify trust gaps and starts conversations about expectations and perceptions.

3. Strengths & Weaknesses Exchange

Each team member shares one strength they bring to the team and one area where they need support. The exercise encourages vulnerability and mutual support and can be completed in conjunction with personality profiling tools such as Insights Discovery, DISC, Myers-Briggs and/or CliftonStrengths.

4. What's Your Leadership Style?

Each person describes how they like to give and receive feedback, how they handle conflict and their decision-making style. The conversation clarifies the team's working preferences and reduces misunderstandings.

5. Blindfolded Leadership Challenge

One team member is blindfolded while the rest of the team guides them through a task (e.g. navigating an obstacle course, assembling a structure, etc). The exercise reinforces trust in team communication and reliance on others.

6. Feedback Circles: Start, Stop, Continue

Each team member gives structured "Start, Stop, Continue" feedback to their peers.

Start: Something they should be doing.

Stop: Something that hinders them.

Continue: A strength they should maintain.

This encourages direct, constructive conversations in a psychologically safe environment. This exercise works well in a retreat setting with a facilitator.

7. Deep Dive One-on-Ones

Rotate structured one-on-one meetings with each leader, focusing on what motivates them, what they need to succeed and their biggest leadership challenge.

The exercise helps break down silos and build more specific personal connections. Again, this exercise works well in a retreat setting with input from a facilitator.

8. Scenario-Based Problem Solving

Present the team with a complex real-world business challenge and have them collaborate to solve it. The exercise helps build trust in decision-making and problem-solving capabilities. The exercise could be facilitated, observed or video-recorded to extract learning about how individuals work as a team and explore dynamics.

9. "Two Truths and a Lie": The Leadership Edition

Each leader shares two true leadership experiences and one fabricated one. This exercise lightens the mood. It also often uncovers hidden stories and promotes a deeper understanding of motivations and behaviour.

10. "Vulnerability Poker"

A thought-provoking card game that encourages vulnerability and builds emotional trust, as each participant is dealt cards that invite sharing around themes such as failures, risks taken, biggest fears, blind spots or leadership lessons. The poker format encourages others to "raise" with a deeper disclosure, whilst the format helps keep the conversation light to normalise vulnerability, strengthen trust and break through the guarded behaviours that often limit executive team cohesion.

For maximum impact, these exercises should be embedded in an ongoing SLT development programme rather than be a feature of a one-off event. As indicated, a skilled facilitator can help ensure psychological safety and guide the team towards real breakthroughs in trust and collaborations that enable:

- Open communication without fear of judgment

- Consistency and reliability that builds confidence in the team

- Clear expectations on how each member contributes to the team's success

- Vulnerability that helps to humanise relationships and build empathy

- Celebrating success together to reinforce a sense of unity and collective accomplishment

- Conflict resolution methods that focus on finding solutions rather than placing blame

- Leadership by example, where leaders play a critical role in setting the tone for trust within the team and demonstrate trustworthiness, integrity and ethical behaviour

However uncomfortable or strange it may sound, especially among experienced senior people, investing time and energy in team-building activities rarely fails to deliver increased collaboration, communication and understanding among the team. Such activities and "games" can be fun and relaxing, and as people relax, they are inclined to reveal more. The alternative is to accept a much more gradual process that will likely fail to optimise the talents sat around the room, as much of what is not revealed or not shared never sees the light of day.

Shared Values

Establishing shared values within an SLT is crucial for alignment, decision-making and driving a cohesive organisational culture. Shared values create a north star that aligns leadership and staff, ensuring everyone is working towards the same end. Whatever the challenge or phase of a business's development, shared values maintain focus during growth, change or crisis. Defining shared values is not just about words on a wall. It's about embedding principles into every decision, behaviour and interaction to drive sustainable success. When done well, shared values create a high-trust, high-performance organisation that thrives in any environment, as they clearly outline and lend legitimacy to the desired behaviours.

However, before a team can align on shared values and ensure authenticity, it is essential to understand what each SLT team member personally values.

> **Exercise:** Have each leader list their top five personal and professional values (e.g. consistency, trailblazer, "do what you say").

Discuss: Identify overlaps and key differences. This helps surface what really matters to the team and defines the non-negotiables for the business.

In a nutshell, shared values are the fundamental principles that should never be compromised when leading a business, and they take priority when driving standards, expected behaviour and decision-making. As a discussion around individual values morphs into company non-negotiables, it should be possible to distil a list of 3 to 5 core leadership values. It is best if the values are specific and actionable (e.g. instead of "respect," say "we challenge ideas, not people"), and the values are documented with crisp, clear descriptions and the accompanying expected behaviours.

Shared values come into their own on real strategic decisions that have long-term consequences. It is worth stress-testing whether those values align with leadership actions. SLT leaders should be encouraged to call out when decisions support or contradict the agreed shared values, and to commit to further refining the values if they prove impractical or misaligned. When finalised, the shared values should form the cornerstone of leadership practices:

Hiring and promotion. Evaluate new leaders based on their understanding of alignment with shared values.

Meeting culture. Reinforce values through leadership behaviours in discussions.

Recognition and accountability. Openly recognise "values-driven" actions and address any misalignments.

By intentionally building shared values collaboratively, testing them in real-world situations and embedding them in leadership behaviours, an SLT can create a foundation of trust, alignment and purpose-driven leadership throughout an organisation.

I recommend using a simple profiling tool from Patrick Lencioni's *The Advantage* on shared values to ensure that what you arrive at is distinctive, compelling and truly reflects the essence of what the business is about.[1]

Lencioni's tool distinguishes between four types of shared values:

Core values. These are a few behavioural traits that lie at the very heart of an organisation. They speak to its core identity and are not contrived.

Aspirational values. These are characteristics the organisation wants to have and wishes it had already. The SLT believes that these are values the organisation must develop to maximise its opportunities in the current market environment.

Permission to play values. These are the bare minimum behavioural and ethical standards required in an organisation. They are universal baseline expectations (e.g. honesty, integrity and respect) that are not unique or differentiating.

Accidental values. These values have appeared, due to neglect or oversight, and do not serve the organisation well.

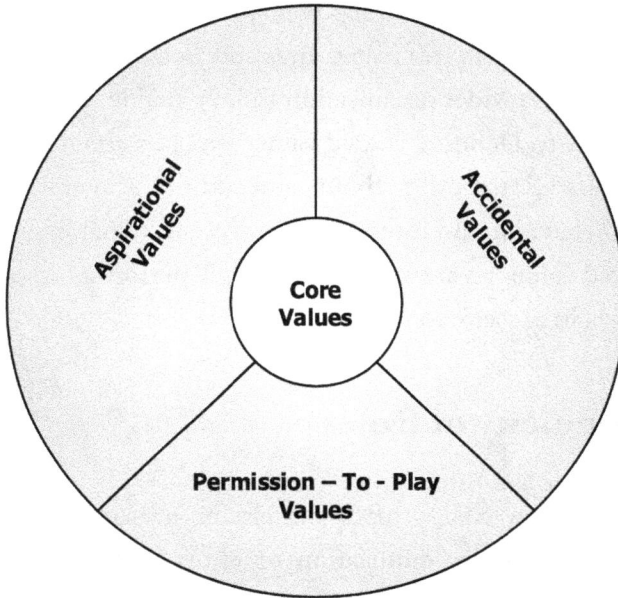

We have all seen when positive shared values can drive performance. I once worked in a creative agency where discretionary effort was gladly given because of individual alignment with what was being built, as well as the outstanding reputation the firm had established in the market. Everybody instinctively shared a will to work hard to keep the firm at the front of a chasing pack, driven by a sense of shared ambition. However, the "work hard, play hard" passion that distinguished the firm's credo drove exceptional performance that was frequently rewarded and celebrated. Interestingly, no posters extolling the virtues of "work hard, play hard" could be found on the walls anywhere in the office, but this value was profoundly felt by all.

By contrast, there are many organisations where values are just words on a wall and rarely observed, if at all. Rather, what one sees is a big budget spent with a corporate identity agency and little to no energy invested in living up to what has been produced. Even lip service feels painful. Shared values are created and modelled by the SLTs, who more often engage the wider organisation to help define the foundations of a firm's identity. Defining shared values isn't just about going through the motions. Rather, it's about embedding principles into every decision, behaviour and interaction to drive sustainable success. Done well, shared values create a high-trust, high-performance organisation that thrives in any environment.

Synchronicity of Roles

High-performing SLTs thrive on clarity of roles. Without clear definitions, confusion, duplication of effort and misalignment can undermine decision-making and execution, consuming wasteful hours of politicking and jostling for position.

Clearly understood roles that mesh well are essential to prevent leadership overlaps and gaps. When roles are clearly defined, SLT leaders focus on their core accountabilities without stepping on each other's toes. It also ensures that no critical functions (e.g. strategy, finance, operations or people development) are neglected and that competencies are developed and deployed to reflect the requirements of the business strategy.

Time spent ensuring clarity in roles is rewarded with enhanced decision-making as each leader knows who is responsible for what, resulting in faster and more confident decision-making. The process of establishing clarity eliminates the "Who owns this?" dilemma that slows progress and leads to finger-pointing and blame shifting if and when things unravel.

When well-defined, the roles that SLT leaders fulfil naturally align leadership with business goals. A well-structured SLT ensures that every critical business function has a leader driving it forward, supported by processes that prevent misalignment between strategy and execution by assigning ownership of key priorities. By clarifying and agreeing on roles at the outset, leaders do not waste time debating ownership or duplicating efforts to increase efficiency. Rather, focusing on the challenge of enhancing the quality of execution helps to detail decision rights and how they apply, enabling other teams in the organisation to move faster, bolder and smarter with more confidence.

When roles are clearly understood, leaders collaborate more effectively and instinctively respect each other's domains. Role clarity reduces friction by setting clear boundaries and expectations, avoiding siloed thinking and highlighting key points of integration across departments. Over time, as collaboration builds, SLT leaders come to trust that their peers will deliver in their areas of responsibility.

Clear role definitions also create a strong foundation for structured leadership development and effective talent progression within a function or business unit. When responsibilities are clearly articulated and expectations are transparent, succession planning becomes more straightforward, with the necessary competencies easier to identify and develop. This may be further strengthened by building leadership capability across disciplines and, in larger organisations, through cross-divisional experience.

There are two key factors for success in defining clear roles in the SLT:

1. **Define and document responsibilities.** Use a RACI matrix (Responsible, Accountable, Consulted, Informed) to clarify roles. Focus debate on establishing decision-making authority by clarifying who has the final say in different areas.

2. **Encourage open conversations.** Create a space for leaders to address role concerns, and as the business needs change and strategy evolves, regularly review roles to stay on point.

By establishing clear roles, an SLT creates a high-functioning leadership dynamic that drives business success, fosters trust and is a key contributor to achieving the seemingly elusive goal of seamless execution.

A Case Study of *Star Trek: The Original Series'* "The Dream Team"

The main four characters in *Star Trek*, often referred to as the "perfect team," are Captain James T. Kirk, Mr Spock, Dr Leonard "Bones" McCoy and Chief Engineer Montgomery "Scotty" Scott.

They are often regarded as a "dream team" because they share:

Diverse skill sets. Each character brings a unique set of skills and expertise to the team. Captain Kirk is a visionary leader, skilled in diplomacy and strategic thinking. Mr. Spock, the Vulcan science officer, provides logical analysis and a cool-headed approach to more detailed planning. Dr. McCoy is an exceptional physician, offering medical expertise and a compassionate viewpoint. Scotty is a deep systems expert who continues to focus on what is needed in the tightest of situations.

Complementary personalities. The four characters have distinct personalities which complement each other. Captain Kirk is adventurous and risk-taking, balancing Spock's logical and analytical nature. McCoy's emotional and often sceptical outlook provides a counterpoint to Spock's logical detachment. Scotty delivers in pragmatic terms whatever is needed and when, and is always working hard to support the USS Enterprise and all her crew.

Trust and friendship. Throughout their voyages on the Starship Enterprise, these characters form deep bonds of trust and friendship. They rely on one another and have proven their loyalty and commitment to each other's well-being time and again. This trust allows them to work seamlessly as a team and face challenges together.

Balance of perspectives. The characters represent different perspectives, often engaging in lively debates. Spock's logic clashes with McCoy's emotional approach, creating a balance between reason and compassion. This dynamic makes for well-rounded decision-making and problem-solving.

Collaboration and adaptability. The four main characters demonstrate a remarkable ability to collaborate and adapt to various situations. They combine their individual strengths and work as a cohesive unit to overcome challenges, whether it's navigating unknown territories or resolving complex conflicts. Their collective skills and flexibility make them highly effective in a wide range of scenarios.

The "dream team" are joined by a strong supporting cast of characters who are a more than competent fit for their roles, such as Lieutenant Nyota Uhura (Communications Officer), Pavel Chekov (Navigation), Hikaru Sulu (Helmsman and Pilot) and others.

The crew of *Star Trek* offers a compelling analogy for an SLT. Each character brings distinct personality traits, perspectives and problem-solving styles that often clash, sometimes collide, but are always united by a shared mission. Their voyages are not smooth sailing; they are filled with unknowns, high-stakes decisions and moments where one part of the team struggles to understand the other.

Just like an SLT, they face new and unfamiliar challenges in every episode. Conflict is inevitable; disagreement is part of the process. What sets them apart is not perfect harmony, but the ability to collaborate under pressure, adapt quickly and trust one another even when the path forward is unclear. The dream team doesn't always know how they will succeed. They simply commit to figuring it out together. It is these qualities that make them a dream team. Not certainty, but collective confidence and mutual reliance "to boldly go" in the face of the unknown.

Shared Goals

I have yet to find any evidence that contradicts the view that a highly effective SLT must have a shared understanding of the company's long-term vision and purpose. When a shared understanding of purpose is lacking, goal setting becomes fragmented as leaders pull in different directions. A key role of the MD/CEO is to provide the overall strategic context and strategic priorities for the business and engage with each SLT leader to address any perceived doubts or challenges to the overall direction of travel.

At a minimum, the SLT should participate in an annual strategic review of objectives and priorities to assess the business vision and purpose, ensuring alignment with the company's overarching vision. This review will include an assessment of current and recent market and business performance, and profile potential after identifying major business challenges and opportunities.

Structured brainstorming exercises should ideally result in agreement on 3 to 5 major strategic themes for the business to address, translating key influential themes into goals and defining clear, outcome-based objectives. Goals may be prioritised by using ranking or voting methods, such as MoSCoW (more on this later), or the impact versus effort matrices, to focus on what matters most and ensure cross-functional buy-in by identifying and addressing potential conflicts and trade-offs to avoid silos.

Once goals are defined and agreed upon, metrics and accountability can be defined and allocated.

Increasingly, I advocate that key results and outcomes for each goal be specifically defined, so that "what is done" when the goal is achieved is clear and unambiguous. Such practices help to build self-managing teams, which may be a desirable shift beyond the SLT. However, accountability must not be lost, and an SLT leader is assigned for each goal to ensure that progress is tracked and any potential risks and barriers are overcome, leading to practical actions being taken.

Once the above steps have been completed and the SLT has strongly confirmed its buy-in and consent, then communication can begin to ensure clear messaging across teams and translate shared goals into department-specific objectives. To ensure ongoing alignment to defined shared goals, I advocate a regular cadence (see Chapter 8):

Monthly leadership check-ins that include quick updates to track goal progress.

Quarterly strategy reviews to adjust objectives based on business shifts.

Annual strategy resets to reflect, refine and set new goals for the following year.

MoSCoW Explained

MoSCoW is a prioritisation framework used to categorise and rank goals based on their importance. It helps senior teams focus on what truly matters by breaking priorities into four categories:

M – Must Have, or non-negotiable. Essential for success; without these, an initiative will fail.

S – Should Have, or high priority but not critical. Important but not absolutely essential; can be implemented later if needed.

C – Could Have, or nice to have. Enhancements that would improve outcomes but are not necessary.

W – Won't Have, or not this time. Low-priority items that are not needed now and can be deferred or dropped.

Why Use MoSCoW?

Ensures alignment. It helps leadership teams agree on what really matters.

Prevents scope creep. It stops distractions by deferring non-essential work.

Drives focus and execution. It keeps teams working on high-impact priorities.

The use of the MoSCoW method would have brought clarity and alignment early in the Airbus project. By collaboratively defining "must-haves" such as core system architecture, interfaces and language protocols, both teams would have agreed on the non-negotiables. "Should haves" and "could haves" would then allow for local flexibility while maintaining overall compatibility. Crucially, agreeing on "won't haves" could have prevented teams from independently pursuing features that risked divergence. This structured prioritisation would have promoted shared understanding, reduced assumptions and kept the teams focused on common goals. As a creative problem-solving tool, MoSCoW encourages discussion, negotiation and clarity, which is exactly what was missing in the cross-border collaboration. Used well, it might have transformed a fragmented development effort into a more cohesive, aligned and ultimately successful project.

SLT Charter

A SLT Charter is a foundational agreement that defines the team's identity, purpose and ways of working. More than a set of rules, the charter is a shared commitment crafted by the SLT that aligns members around common expectations, values and behaviours. A charter serves the purpose of confirming an SLT's identity as well as acting as a compass and a mirror, guiding decision-making and collaboration, while reflecting the collective strengths and responsibilities of those around the table. In short, it brings "stuff out into the open" in a way that facilitates a constructive discussion about how the team can operate at its best.

At its core, the SLT Charter clarifies why the team exists beyond individual roles and outlines the strategic value it adds to the organisation, as well as how it fosters coherence across functions. It articulates the team's collective purpose, the outcomes it is accountable for and how success will be measured.

A charter also defines how the SLT works together. It typically includes agreed norms for communication, decision-making, conflict resolution and mutual accountability. Importantly, it recognises the unique contributions of each member, highlighting not just their functional expertise but also the perspectives, behaviours and leadership qualities they bring to the whole.

By creating the charter together, team members build a shared sense of ownership and increase their sense of collective identity. The process of creating a charter strengthens trust and provides an all-important reference point in times of tension or drift. A well-used SLT Charter is not static; it evolves with the team, and is periodically reviewed to stay relevant as the organisation's context changes. In doing so, it helps the team stay aligned, connected and focused on what matters most together.

Home Truths

There's a quiet power in home truths. The simple, unvarnished insights that often sit in plain sight but are easily overlooked. They're not complex theories or grand revelations, but rather the kind of truths that land with a thud of recognition because, deep down, we already know them. Their strength lies in their clarity and directness. Home truths cut through noise and pretence, reminding us of what really matters and challenging us to live and lead with greater honesty, responsibility and alignment. They may be uncomfortable at times, but they are rarely unkind, and often, they're exactly what we need to hear.

The home truths of what makes for a highly effective SLT are:

Challenge assumptions regularly. SLT leaders must question their own thinking, as well as that of others. There is no substitute for the raw power of "heavy-duty" thinking. Do not misplace reliance on an AI chatbot.

Establish a culture of honesty. Senior leaders must welcome bad news early and not suppress uncomfortable truths. SLT leaders listen deeply and reflect on what they hear.

Keep it professional. Trying to be best friends with colleagues can blur boundaries, complicate decisions and make it harder to lead. You don't need to be liked by everyone to be effective, but you do need to be fair, consistent and kind. Professional warmth extends beyond personal closeness when it comes to building strong, sustainable teams.

Alignment is more important than hierarchy. If the SLT, product, commercial and operational teams are not aligned, execution will suffer. Clarity is reinforced through regular check-ins to address the risk of misalignment early.

Speed wins. A slow-moving SLT kills competitive advantage. Delayed decisions are often worse than wrong decisions.

Clarity brings focus. Clarity isn't just about information. It's about alignment, commitment and confidence in execution. Clarity is the source of foundational alignment for team participants.

Roles are owned. Every member knows their role and how their contribution fits into the bigger picture. Clarity of who owns which decisions avoids paralysis and delays, while consulting and informing avoids surprises and a lack of coordination.

What "done "looks like. SLTs define what success looks like in specific, concrete terms. Critical decisions, objectives and action steps are also recorded to remove ambiguity.

Summary

Foundational alignment is essential for a high-performing SLT. It starts with building strong interpersonal connections through openness and vulnerability, which fosters trust and productive dialogue. Clarifying shared values strengthens this alignment by defining not only what the team is trying to achieve but also how they work together. A clear set of distinctive values guides behaviour, decision-making and talent fit – especially under pressure.

Clarity of roles and how they integrate is equally critical. When responsibilities are well-defined and interdependent, the team avoids confusion and duplication, enabling faster decisions and stronger accountability. Alongside this, shared goals ensure alignment across functions, promoting collaboration and a focus on enterprise-wide success rather than siloed interests.

An SLT charter formalises this alignment. It sets out the team's purpose, behavioural expectations, decision-making norms, meeting rhythms and accountability mechanisms. More than a static document, it serves as an ongoing reference point that helps the team stay grounded, especially during times of tension or change.

Reflective Questions

The questions set out below are designed to help you internalise key ideas, examine your own experiences in light of what you've read and consider how any insights might shape your thinking and actions in future. There are no right answers, only honest ones. Use these opportunities to reflect to deepen your awareness, spark conversation with others or simply increase awareness of what's changing for you as you make progress through this book. The questions are:

Are we setting aside time to build relationships and strengthen team trust?

How do we hold each other accountable to our shared values, especially when it's difficult?

What one conversation about roles and responsibilities would help improve how we work together?

How do we check and recalibrate our shared goals as conditions change?

What does success look like for this leadership team in the next 12 to 18 months?

There is a longer list of questions in the "Appendix: Reflective Questions." These are designed to be addressed when you, with or without the team, have more time available for reflection, rather than reaction.

Chapter 3
Happiness and Productivity

"Happiness is not just a mood. It's a work ethic."
– Shawn Achor, Author

"The wonderful thing about true laughter is that it just destroys any kind of system for dividing people."
– John Cleese, Actor and Comedian

Over the years I spent as an SLT member, it became apparent that the most productive teams had the most fun. The teams that grind away, work the hours and produce the goods may be financially effective, but they are joyless. I've also served time there. These teams endure churn and instability. It stands to reason that there is no real contest when it comes to choosing where you would rather spend time.

I grew up in a Scottish Calvinist environment where it was "work, rest, then play" in that order. As it turns out, the most productive senior teams "play, work and rest." It takes extra effort to overcome bias and shift one's mindset to adopt an intuitively contrary approach to working. After all, it is a common belief that the hard work that won the place at the "top table" is the very thing that will sustain you and your peers. It certainly helps, but hard work is not what makes the difference, and making a difference is why teams exist.

This chapter explores the growing body of evidence showing how happiness fuels productivity, creativity and resilience. It connects insights from neuroscience, behavioural psychology and organisational performance to what many great leaders have known intuitively: People do their best work when they feel valued, trusted and inspired. Whether it's stronger collaboration, sharper problem-solving or lower turnover, the business case for happiness is no longer anecdotal. It's measurable.

The chapter also introduces the concept of a "Happiness Manifesto" for SLTs. It offers practical ways to build a culture where people feel safe, purposeful and proud of the impact they make. When leaders prioritise happiness, not as an afterthought but as a core strategy, businesses don't just perform better. Happy businesses are simply better places to be.

The Science of Happiness and Productivity

Happiness is not just a subjective emotional state; it has tangible effects on the brain and body that directly enhance productivity. Studies in neuroscience have shown that happiness activates the prefrontal cortex, which is responsible for problem-solving, decision-making and cognitive flexibility. Positive emotions also stimulate the release of dopamine and serotonin, neurotransmitters associated with motivation and focus.

A well-known study conducted by economists at the University of Warwick found that happiness increases productivity by an average of 12% and can reach up to 20% in certain cases.[1] In their experiment, participants who were exposed to positive stimuli, such as comedy clips or receiving small rewards, performed significantly better on cognitive tasks than those in a neutral or negative emotional state. Research by Shawn Achor, a leading expert on positive psychology, reinforces this point. His book, *The Happiness Advantage*, presents findings that employees who cultivate positive emotions are not only more productive but also more resilient in the face of challenges.[2] According to Achor, happiness precedes success because a positive mindset enhances creativity, problem-solving abilities and adaptability, which are all essential traits for workplace efficiency.

Happiness in the workplace leads to higher levels of engagement and motivation. Engaged employees are those who feel emotionally invested in their work and are willing to go above and beyond to contribute to the organisation's success. Gallup's *State of the Global Workplace Report* for 2021 and 2025 found that employees who report high levels of well-being are significantly more engaged. Engaged employees show a 17% increase in productivity compared to disengaged employees.[3]

Self-determination theory also highlights the importance of intrinsic motivation, where individuals perform tasks for personal satisfaction rather than external rewards.[4] Happiness fosters intrinsic motivation by making work feel more meaningful and enjoyable. When employees feel valued, supported and excited about their work, they are naturally more driven to excel.

Happiness enhances cognitive function, leading to greater creativity and problem-solving abilities. Positive emotions broaden an individual's thought-action repertoire, allowing them to consider more possibilities and develop innovative solutions.[5] A study published in the *Journal of Applied Psychology* found that employees in a positive mood are more likely to engage in creative thinking and generate novel ideas.[6]

Creativity is essential in fast-paced and competitive work environments. Companies that prioritise employee happiness benefit from increased innovation and the ability to adapt to change more effectively. Google has long been recognised for its commitment to employee well-being, offering programmes that promote work-life balance and personal growth. The company's emphasis on a positive work culture has significantly contributed to its sustained success as one of the world's most innovative tech giants.

A happy work environment fosters better relationships between colleagues, leading to increased collaboration and team performance. Emma Seppala and Kim Cameron published research in the *Harvard Business Review* that suggests positive workplace relationships improve communication, trust and teamwork.[7] Employees who experience positive emotions are more likely to support their co-workers, share knowledge and work together harmoniously toward common goals. Additionally, organisations with a culture of happiness experience lower turnover rates.

According to a study by the Society for Human Resource Management, companies that invest in employee well-being experience 25% lower turnover than those that neglect workplace happiness.[8] The retention of skilled employees reduces recruitment and training costs while maintaining a stable and experienced workforce.

Workplace stress is a major barrier to productivity, leading to burnout, absenteeism and decreased performance. The American Institute of Stress reports that job stress costs US businesses an estimated $300 billion annually due to lost productivity and healthcare expenses.[9] Work undertaken by AXA UK estimated that "poor mind health" costs the UK economy £103 billion.[10]

Happiness acts as a protective buffer against stress, improving employees' resilience and ability to cope with workplace challenges. When employees experience positive emotions, they are better equipped to manage pressure, recover from setbacks and maintain focus. A longitudinal study by Diener and Seligman found that individuals with high levels of life satisfaction exhibit better stress management skills and overall well-being, which in turn enhances their professional performance.[11]

The Business Case for Happiness

From a business perspective, encouraging happiness in the workplace leads to measurable improvements in financial performance. A 2019 study by the UK's Department for Business, Energy & Industrial Strategy found that companies with high employee well-being outperform their competitors in terms of revenue growth, customer satisfaction and innovation.[12] Companies that prioritise happiness have reaped tangible rewards. Salesforce, consistently ranked as one of the best places to work, has experienced increased employee engagement and revenue growth due to its emphasis on a positive work culture. Similarly, online shoe retailer Zappos, now part of Amazon, attributes much of its success to its commitment to employee happiness, demonstrating that a thriving work environment leads to better customer service and profitability. *Delivering Happiness*, a book written by the founder of Zappos, the late Tony Hsieh, provides a stimulating perspective on creating a lively and fun work environment that focuses on delivering the best possible customer experience.[13]

In summary, the idea that productivity leads to happiness is a misconception. Instead, the evidence strongly suggests that happiness is the foundation upon which productivity is built. Scientific research in psychology and organisational behaviour demonstrates that when people at work are happy, they experience enhanced cognitive function, increased motivation, greater creativity and improved interpersonal relationships. This all leads to higher engagement, lower stress levels and better overall performance.

SLTs and the organisations that recognise and act on the importance of workplace happiness benefit from increased innovation, lower turnover and higher financial success. Forward-thinking leadership teams invest in employee well-being, foster a positive work culture and emphasise happiness as a core fundamental of people development strategy.

An SLT "Happiness Manifesto"

Promoting happiness in the modern post-COVID workplace requires intentional leadership practices that prioritise connection, purpose and employee well-being. It takes a different kind of boldness and courage to be vulnerable and embrace the "softer" side of people management. An SLT is uniquely placed to lead the way and set the tone for workplace climate by working through, as funding and resources allow, the implementation of a "happiness manifesto" based around the following influential themes.

Foster Psychological Safety and Trust

Encourage open communication and create a culture where employees feel safe to voice concerns, share ideas and take risks without fear of retribution. Do not shoot the messenger!

Promote transparency by maintaining a drumbeat of regularly sharing company updates, challenges and decisions openly. Share both "good news" and avoid sugar coating the "bad news."

Normalise discussions around mental health and well-being. Demonstrate understanding and display empathy.

Celebrate silliness and deflate the self-important. One business I worked with created an annual "alternative Christmas magazine" put together by volunteer staff. It resembled a hastily constructed school magazine made up of newspaper headlines, adapted cut-outs and edited cartoons. It was hilarious to read and sometimes humbling to absorb. It brought everybody down to the same level and built social connections. When it was distributed in the office, all work for the day stopped and it signalled the start of Christmas. A good laugh heals a lot of hurts.

Prioritise Work-Life Balance and Flexibility

Offer hybrid or remote work options that align with the business's work patterns and accommodate different working styles and preferences. If you go down this route, be clear about the days and reasons why everybody is expected to attend the workplace.

Invest in workplace facilities that create a sense of destination by recognising and supporting the busy lives of working mothers/couples with flexible time, catering and transforming otherwise "dead space" into activity zones. I have seen previously stuffy and conservative workplaces transformed by converting excess space into a small gym for a very modest outlay.

Encourage employees to take breaks and use their holiday time throughout the year, and not in one "splurge" during the last few weeks of the "holiday year."

Trial "no meeting" days and flexible scheduling to guard against burnout and loss of productivity.

Recognise and Celebrate Achievements

Regularly acknowledge employees' contributions through public appreciation, rewards or bonuses.

Implement peer-to-peer recognition programmes. "Cheers for peers" can mean as much as awards from seniors in recognising effort, teamwork and excellence.

Celebrate milestones, both personal and professional, to create a sense of community and belonging.

Invest in Employee Development and Growth

Provide ongoing training and development opportunities for all employees and weight spending on individuals according to their position on talent management matrices.

Support career progression with mentoring and coaching for the performers who exhibit the most potential. Make sure the mentor from the SLT makes time to be fully present in the sessions together, as well as allocating time to research what to bring to their mentee when they meet up.

Encourage a "ask once only" culture of learning, accountability and performance built on the foundations of "doing what you say you are going to do" (see Chapter 10). An "ask once only" culture is one where requests, decisions or instructions are clearly communicated, understood and acted upon the first time without the need for chasing, repetition or clarification. It reflects a high-trust, high-accountability environment where people take ownership, follow through reliably and respect each other's time and commitments.

Strengthen Workplace Relationships and Social Connection

Organise team-building activities that comprise both virtual and outdoor immersive experiences to build deeper connections and relationships. Design the activities to ensure that all participants can equally engage, have fun, laugh at themselves and others, and learn something meaningful about how to positively influence team dynamics during the time spent together.

Encourage cross-functional collaboration, with job swaps for the "curious" to create a deeper understanding of "how it works here." Explore and sample alternative career paths, and help create a greater sense of shared purpose.

Establish and promote "social huddle" activities that bring people together from all across the business to share and explore hobbies and pastimes of mutual interest, encouraging people to bond on a different level.

Create informal social spaces (e.g. virtual coffee chats or in-office lounges/break-out spaces) that are inviting and relaxing to spend time in.

Promote Health and Well-being

Offer wellness programs, such as fitness challenges, meditation sessions and counselling services from a trusted and qualified Employee Assistance Provider (EAP) to provide confidential support.

Encourage healthy work habits, such as regular physical movement and invest in creating ergonomic workspaces.

Align Work with Purpose and Meaning

Help employees see the bigger picture by connecting their work to the company's mission. Share stories that connect an individual's and a department's output and the difference their specific contribution makes to a customer

Bring the voice of the customer into every corner of the business and ensure that during onboarding, new staff "walk in the customer's shoes" so that they know and feel the significance of the work they are doing. Put in the extra effort to ensure that back office staff are aware of the client issues and challenges the business is seeking to address and solve, so that they can play their part as well.

Support local corporate social responsibility (CSR) initiatives that employees can engage with. Alternatively, sign up to B1G1 (Business for Good at b1g1.com) and make a difference in somebody's life somewhere else on the planet on a cause that is close to employees' hearts, as well as being in step with the business's overall purpose.

Create an Inclusive and Diverse Culture

Ensure fair opportunities for growth and advancement for all. For sure, create a meritocracy where talent rises to the top, but ensure that everybody has a chance to fulfil their role, achieve more and become the best version of themselves.

Actively listen to and address employee concerns related to diversity, equity and inclusion (DEI). Address any perceptions of "lip service" with action.

Promote diverse leadership and representation at all levels, wherever possible, and avoid "tokenism."

The "happiness agenda" cannot be the sole responsibility of one SLT leader, not even the HR Director. When a single function owns it, it risks becoming a side initiative rather than a central driver of performance. Real impact comes when the entire SLT are joined at the hip, fully aligned and committed. By embedding the principles of the "Happiness Manifesto" into a unified, cross-functional approach, SLTs can create a workplace culture where people feel genuinely valued, motivated and connected. It can be a workplace where happiness is not a programme, but a by-product of how the business is led. All of this, in turn, leads to higher engagement and productivity, which transforms performance.

None of this is new. Indeed, a famous case study showcases the Sears Profit model that was developed in the 1990s when Sears was a mature business undergoing a turnaround and forced to explore new pathways to unlock higher levels of profit performance. Sears was the first to document the "Employee-Customer-Profit" model, which illustrated how employee attitudes directly influenced customer satisfaction and, subsequently, financial outcomes.[14] This model demonstrated that a 5% increase in employee engagement led to a 1.3% rise in customer satisfaction, resulting in a 0.5% revenue growth per year, which equated to $250 million annually across the retail estate. Sears went on to introduce Total Performance Indicators (TPIs) to monitor both financial and non-financial metrics, ensuring a more balanced view of organisational health and recognising positive staff behaviours. The approach emphasised the importance of aligning employee satisfaction and empowerment with customer experiences to drive profitability.

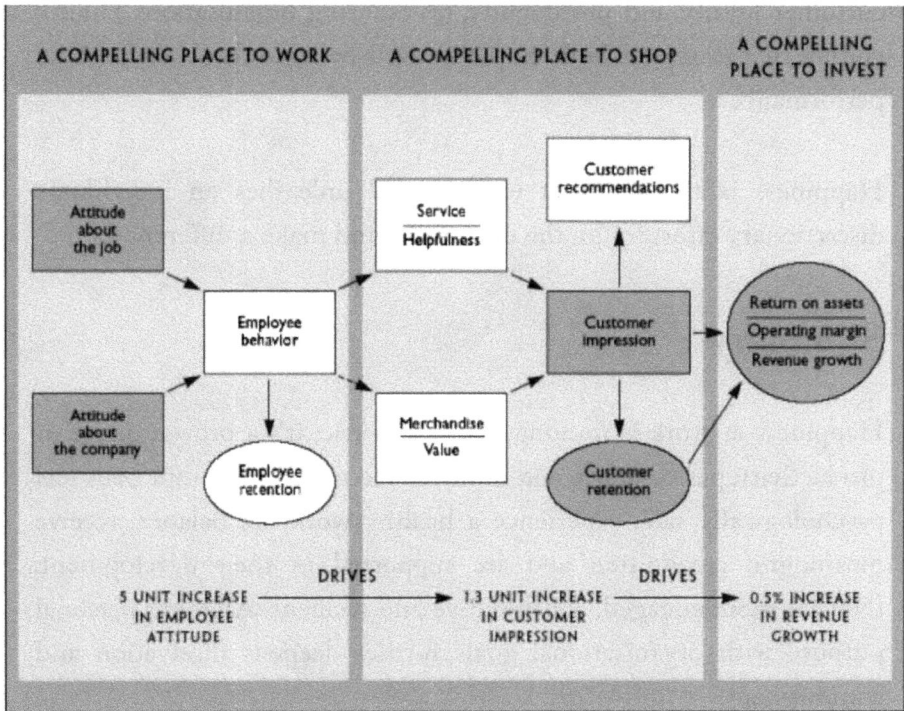

| A COMPELLING PLACE TO WORK | A COMPELLING PLACE TO SHOP | A COMPELLING PLACE TO INVEST |

Attitude about the job → Employee behavior

Attitude about the company → Employee behavior

Employee behavior → Employee retention

Service / Helpfulness

Merchandise / Value

Customer recommendations

Customer impression

Customer retention

Return on assets / Operating margin / Revenue growth

DRIVES

DRIVES

5 UNIT INCREASE IN EMPLOYEE ATTITUDE → 1.3 UNIT INCREASE IN CUSTOMER IMPRESSION → 0.5% INCREASE IN REVENUE GROWTH

Nb. The rectangles represent survey information and the ovals hard data. The measurements in grey are those that are collected and distributed in the form the Sears Total Performance Indicators

The Sears case study highlights that prioritising employee engagement and happiness is not just an HR initiative but a strategic business imperative.

Sears no longer commands the retail world stage. Indeed, in current times, Sears has become a significantly diminished shadow of its former self due to its failure to innovate both online and offline. However, the lessons and insights offered up in its then ground-breaking work have been adopted and adapted by multiple businesses seeking to leverage the intrinsic link between employee engagement, customer loyalty and profitability, by ensuring organisations build a culture that promotes both employee well-being and robust financial performance.

Happiness is the key that unlocks and unleashes an individual's discretionary effort to "go the extra mile" and make a difference.

Summary

Happiness at work is no longer a soft metric; it's a proven driver of productivity, performance and business success. When employees feel psychologically safe, experience a healthy work-life balance, receive meaningful recognition and are supported in their development, they are more engaged, collaborative and resilient. Aligning personal purpose with organisational goals further deepens motivation and commitment.

Multiple research studies have shown a strong correlation between happier teams and higher customer satisfaction, stronger competitiveness and higher levels of successful innovation. Increasingly, forward-thinking firms are measuring employee happiness as a key indicator of organisational health. In short, creating the conditions for happiness at work is not just good for people, it is a self-enlightened interest that makes for smart business.

Measuring happiness at work has become an increasingly popular way to understand team morale and drive performance, but it's not as simple as sending out a survey and expecting insight. To do it well, organisations need to look beyond surface-level sentiment and focus on what really drives lasting engagement: autonomy, psychological safety, recognition and a sense of purpose.

Quantitative tools, such as pulse surveys and eNPS (employee Net Promoter Score), are useful, but they should be balanced with qualitative input, including open comments, listening sessions and team reflections. Happiness is not static, so tracking trends over time is far more meaningful than reacting to a single data point. And importantly, any measurement must be followed by visible action. Employees quickly become cynical if they are asked how they feel but see nothing change.

That said, happiness isn't the same as constant positivity. Challenging work, tough conversations and honest feedback are all part of a healthy, high-performing culture. Treating happiness as a KPI or insisting on cheerfulness can backfire, leading to performative behaviour and suppressed concerns. It's also important to recognise that happiness means different things to different people. What energises one group might well feel alienating to another.

Perhaps most crucially, happiness data should be used as a signal and not an answer. When interpreted thoughtfully and acted upon with care, it can help SLTs create environments where people feel good and do great work.

Reflective Questions

The questions set out below are designed to help you internalise key ideas, examine your own experiences in light of what you've read, and consider how any insights might shape your thinking and actions in future. There are no right answers, only honest ones. Use these opportunities to reflect to deepen your awareness, spark conversation with others, or simply increase awareness of what's changing for you as you make progress through this book.

Do people in our organisation feel safe to speak up, challenge ideas or admit mistakes without fear of blame or judgment?

Are our recognition systems inclusive, or do they unintentionally favour certain roles, personalities or working styles?

What gets in the way of genuine human connection in our culture, and what could we change?

How clearly have we articulated why we do what we do, and how often do we connect day-to-day work to that purpose?

How well do we model the behaviours and values that promote a culture of engagement and well-being?

There is a longer list of questions in the "Appendix: Reflective Questions." These are designed to be addressed when you, with or without the team, have more time available for reflection, rather than reaction.

Chapter 4
Delegate Authority to Empower and Create Leaders

"Great things in business are never done by one person. They are done by a team of people."
– Steve Jobs, Innovator

Leadership is not about holding on to control; it's about knowing when and how to let it go. At the heart of high-performing organisations is a simple truth: Authority that is hoarded stifles initiative, but authority that is shared unlocks potential. This chapter explores why the best senior leaders do not just make decisions – they build decision-makers. By shifting from command-and-control to a culture of trust and intent, they empower others to lead, act and take ownership.

Drawing on real-world experiences, including the powerful case of Captain David Marquet and the USS Santa Fe, the chapter highlights how deliberate delegation – grounded in psychological safety and clarity of purpose – fosters a culture where leadership permeates every level of the business. When people are trusted to make decisions and are equipped to do so, they stop waiting for permission and start leading from their current position.

But empowerment doesn't happen by accident. It requires clear expectations, mutual trust and a shared language for problem-solving. The chapter introduces tools such as the Ladder of Leadership™ and outlines how creative problem-solving methods can hardwire autonomy and initiative into everyday team life. The goal is not just better execution; it's building a resilient organisation where leadership is a collective responsibility and where more people are ready to step up when it matters most.

Leadership on Show

It's the annual conference for the Top 100 most senior managers in the business, hosted in a stylish venue. The conference is not generating any fresh perspectives as it plods along. Consultants are fussing over flipcharts, and the Group CEO has just addressed the room, requesting that participants be open and honest in challenging the business strategy. There are a dozen roundtables where participants are seated, and a facilitator is assigned to each group. Time slips by, and eventually each table is invited to the front of the room to share their observations and recommendations on "what we could do differently."

Suddenly, and unexpectedly, interest levels at the event surge. There is a man at the front of the room speaking passionately about how flawed the current business strategy is and how it is taking the business in the wrong direction. To a hushed audience that gives him rapt attention, he takes the time to detail his critique, outlining specific challenges while adding weight to his arguments by quoting supporting data and spontaneously offering a few added-value observations of his own. When he completes his debrief and eventually sits down, one could literally hear a pin drop.

The Group CEO takes to his feet and moves across to the centre of the stage. Following a short address highlighting recent progress and achievements, he pointedly asks, "Does anybody else here think like John?"

There is no show of hands.

The next speaker steps forward, and the conference resumes. By the end of the day, a few new insights are delicately shared, but nothing of any great substance is tabled as a challenge or divergent point of view – except for the viewpoint that John had succinctly expressed. The Group CEO wraps up the day's discussion, and everybody heads for the exit.

John looks miserable. He had been open and honest, he had spoken up, but nobody is speaking to him now.

The conference centre is a short bus ride from the hotel. The conversation at the bar is animated. Nobody sits with, or even near, John. He is on his own, and he knows it, and he evidently feels the pain before retreating to his room. He had accepted the invitation to challenge but stumbled into the wrong moment to express views that others advised should be done more privately, if at all. John had not read the room. He was unaware of what "open and honest" really meant at this event. He had taken the challenge at face value and been true to himself and his colleagues, but he missed the mark. It was his first and last Top 100 conference with the company. He left the firm within 48 hours. John was "toast" and faded into folklore.

Business life has its many ups and downs. Waste is everywhere, and very often it is found right under one's nose – as in the case of flying 100 senior leaders halfway round the world to come together to review and reset strategy, only for the Group CEO to suppress a discordant voice and send out a chilling message that challenge is neither welcome nor tolerated. The moment became an unfortunate story shared time and again, reinforcing a perception of a company culture characterised by fear, with all the toxic and negative connotations.

Strategies are rarely, if ever, rewritten in rooms with 100 people. At such events, it is more productive to focus on connecting purpose and plan to ensure a shared understanding of strategic priorities through a facilitated session addressing the question, "What does winning look like together?" Alternatively, one could harness the considerable wisdom in the room to tackle real business challenges and form breakout groups to work on a few select enterprise-level issues. A life-long colleague likes to frame such opportunities as "sacrificing holy cows to make the best sizzling steaks!" Or one could be bolder by checking in on company culture to ensure alignment with the leadership behaviours that enable the business strategy to succeed. This can be achieved by asking questions such as "What are we role-modelling?" and "What do we need to leave behind to lead at the next level?" And then, complete the work to ensure clarity on what leaders will take away and act upon.

Many people overthink it, but showing some vulnerability and empathy at a company conference of senior leaders simply requires authenticity, some courage and good intentions towards others. If the objective is to break down barriers and build connections, then senior leaders should leave out rehearsed speeches and glitzy PowerPoint decks and share real stories of challenges, failures and lessons learned.

Another effective approach is to express genuine appreciation for the team and one's colleagues, acknowledging the contributions of others and highlighting where collaboration is essential to success. Design the event to prioritise time for everyone to engage, ask open-ended questions and encourage others to share their experiences, creating an atmosphere where vulnerability is met with respect, not judgment. By intentionally modelling vulnerability, leaders create psychological safety, deepen trust and set a tone where honesty, authenticity and genuine connection become the norm within the organisation. Doing so creates an environment that allows others to flourish.

The Power of Intentional Leadership

David Marquet describes the single most potent example of intentional leadership in his book *Turn the Ship Around*, which is based on his experience as the captain of the USS Santa Fe.[1] This nuclear submarine was ranked at the bottom of the league table for performance of ship and crew in the US Navy when he took his command. His leadership transformation involved shifting from a top-down, "command and control" approach to one of empowerment and distributed decision-making, providing essential lessons on delegation and leadership at all levels.

The Context: A Failing Leadership Model

Before taking command of the USS Santa Fe, Marquet was trained in traditional hierarchical leadership, where decisions flowed from the top and subordinates simply executed orders. He had spent the last year in preparation learning about the Navy's newest class of submarine, only to be assigned to an ancient submarine he was totally unfamiliar with two weeks before taking up his command. It was nearly impossible for him to provide the detailed instructions his crew would be accustomed to receiving. This moment of realisation was sparked by the inability of a senior officer to fulfil an order given by the new captain, which the ship was not designed to perform, and the senior officer merely parroted without challenge. This was a defining moment. Marquet realised that everything he had come to understand about leadership and how it flowed down "from above" just did not apply in the situation he found himself in. After some soul-searching and reflection, he chose to innovate and pursue a radically different approach, empowering his crew to make decisions themselves.

Delegation Through Empowerment: Pushing Authority Down

Marquet introduced a shift from a leader-follower model to a leader-leader structure, where everyone took ownership of their work rather than waiting for orders. A key principle of his leadership philosophy was pushing decision-making authority to the lowest competent level. Instead of giving orders, he encouraged his crew to take initiative and voice their intent.

One of the most instructive practices he introduced was the use of "I intend to…" statements. Rather than waiting for permission or giving direct orders, crew members were expected to communicate their intended actions. So, instead of saying, "What should I do next?" a crew member would say, "I intend to submerge the ship to 400 feet." This subtle shift forced individuals to take responsibility for their actions and increased accountability throughout the organisation. This was later developed into the Ladder of Leadership™ by Marquet, which transitions individuals from passive followers to proactive leaders. It progresses through stages: from waiting for orders ("Tell me what to do"), to expressing observations ("I see…"), sharing thoughts ("I think…"), expressing preferences ("I would like…"), stating intentions ("I intend to…"), reporting actions taken ("I've done…") and finally, autonomous operation ("I've been doing…"). This approach changes conversations while growing an individual's confidence and capability through empowerment, enabling responsible decision-making at the lowest level of an organisation.

Engaging individuals through conversation and informed questioning, supplemented by affirmations, reflective listening and tactful summarising, rather than directive telling, significantly enhances the motivation to assume responsibility for one's actions.

- Questions encourage individuals to reflect on their thinking and personal insights

- Affirmations recognise and reinforce the individual's strengths and efforts, which build confidence and self-belief

- Reflective listening demonstrates empathy through understanding and echoes individual statements

- Summarising consolidates the discussion to ensure mutual understanding

By utilising these conversational techniques, individuals are guided to articulate their own reasons for change, resulting in a greater sense of ownership and responsibility over their decisions and actions.

Ladder of Leadership™

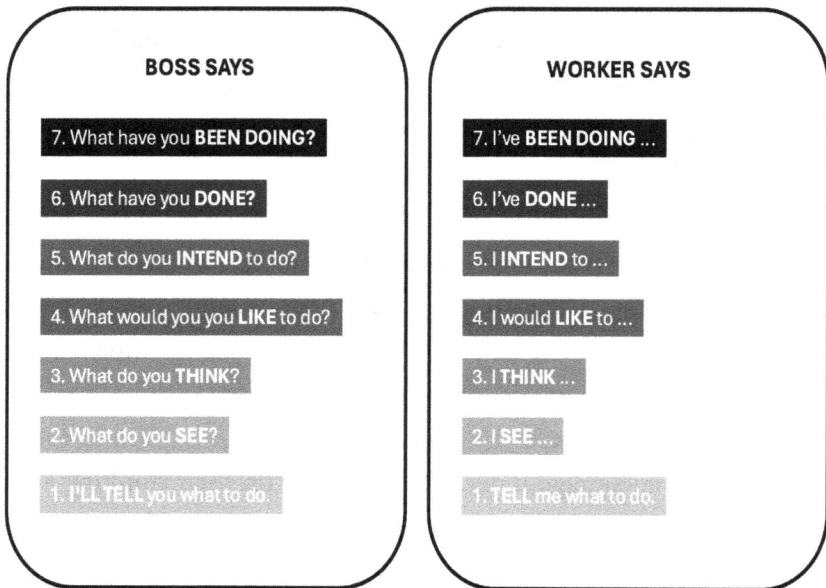

BOSS SAYS	WORKER SAYS
7. What have you **BEEN DOING?**	7. I've **BEEN DOING** ...
6. What have you **DONE?**	6. I've **DONE** ...
5. What do you **INTEND** to do?	5. I **INTEND** to ...
4. What would you you **LIKE** to do?	4. I would **LIKE** to ...
3. What do you **THINK?**	3. I **THINK** ...
2. What do you **SEE?**	2. I **SEE** ...
1. I'LL **TELL** you what to do.	1. **TELL** me what to do.

Eliminating the Need for Permission

Marquet deliberately moved away from the traditional model where subordinates seek approval before taking action. Instead, he focused on giving control rather than taking control. This was not a reckless transfer of authority; it was a calculated empowerment based on ensuring competence and clarity.

Competence. Marquet ensured that his crew had the necessary knowledge and training to make informed decisions. He invested heavily in developing his team's technical expertise, so they had the confidence to act independently.

Clarity. He made sure that everyone understood the broader mission of the ship, not just their individual tasks. When people understood the "why" behind their work, they were able to make better decisions on their own.

This approach transformed the culture on the USS Santa Fe from one of passive compliance to proactive leadership at every level.

Breaking Away from the Leader-Follower Mindset

Traditionally, organisations operate on a leader-follower model, where one person makes decisions, and others simply execute them. This creates bottlenecks, slows down operations and reduces engagement. Marquet replaced this with the leader-leader model, in which every individual is encouraged to take responsibility for their own role as a leader.

By trusting his crew and delegating responsibility, Marquet created a culture where individuals were expected to think critically and act decisively. Over time, this shift led to a remarkable transformation that culminated in the Santa Fe ranking as the highest-performing submarine in the US Navy.

The Role of Psychological Safety in Delegation

A key factor in the success of Marquet's approach was psychological safety, creating an environment where people felt safe to speak up, take initiative and even challenge the status quo without fear of punishment.

One way he fostered psychological safety was by eliminating fear-driven leadership. He recognised that in traditional naval leadership, subordinates feared making mistakes, leading to a culture of silence and blind obedience. By shifting the dynamic, he encouraged open discussion, learning from mistakes and constructive feedback, which empowered his crew to take ownership of their actions.

The Long-Term Impact: A Sustainable Leadership Model

Marquet's transformation of Santa Fe had lasting effects that extended beyond his tenure. His leadership philosophy ensured that improvements in performance and morale were not dependent on him as an individual but were instead embedded in the culture of the submarine.

The Santa Fe's crew members continued to thrive even after Marquet left, with many going on to take leadership roles elsewhere in the Navy. This demonstrated that effective empowerment and delegation create a self-sustaining leadership model rather than one reliant on a single charismatic figure at the top.

Key Lessons in Delegation and Empowerment

Marquet's experience provides practical takeaways for senior leadership team (SLT) leaders looking to delegate more effectively and create a culture of empowerment that:

Shifts from permission-seeking to intent-based leadership, encouraging team members to express their intentions instead of waiting for approval. This builds confidence and accountability.

Pushes authority down to the lowest competent level by delegating decision-making to those closest to where the work is performed, while ensuring they have the necessary knowledge and training.

Creates clarity around the business mission and objectives, enabling individuals to gain a deeper understanding of the bigger picture and make more informed, independent decisions.

Ensures competence through learning and training. People can only be empowered when they have the skills to handle responsibility effectively.

Embraces psychological safety that encourages open dialogue, making it safe to challenge ideas and eliminate fear-based leadership.

Builds a leader-leader culture by moving away from command-and-control to developing leaders at all levels so that the business does not rely on a single person at the top.

Marquet's experience demonstrates that true leadership is not about giving orders but about building competence, providing control and creating clarity that allows every team member to act as a leader in their own right.[2] This approach to delegation is not only a more efficient use of resources that improves performance, but it also builds a more resilient, engaged and high-performing organisation.

Creative Problem Solving is the DNA of Empowerment

Infusing an organisation with a creative problem-solving methodology that evolves into a shared, common language is pivotal for fostering a culture of innovation, facilitating effective delegation, and empowering employees. Encoded within any creative problem-solving approach are the building blocks that boost an organisation's adaptability, as well as strengthen collaboration and decision-making processes.

All creative problem-solving methodologies offer structured frameworks for quickly identifying the core of a problem and developing effective solutions. Approaches are typically structured over three stages: 1) understanding the problem, 2) generating ideas and 3) moving to action planning for implementing selected solutions.[3] When a chosen creative problem-solving methodology takes root and evolves an established shared language within an organisation, it brings people together to express and explore diverse approaches to tackling problems, while ensuring overall consistency and coherence in approach.

Embedding creative problem-solving into the organisational culture encourages continuous innovation. Employees are more likely to propose novel ideas and challenge the status quo when there is a recognised and clear shared process to guide their creativity. This culture shift transforms the organisation into a dynamic entity that proactively seeks improvements and adapts to changing environments.

Creative problem-solving simplifies delegation by providing clear guidelines on how tasks should be approached and executed. Leaders can assign responsibilities with confidence, knowing that employees have the tools and understanding to tackle challenges independently. This clarity reduces micromanagement and enables leaders to focus on strategic initiatives by trusting their teams to handle operational issues effectively.

When employees are equipped with a creative problem-solving framework, they gain confidence in their ability to address challenges. This empowerment leads to increased job satisfaction and motivation, as individuals feel valued and more capable of achieving their goals. Empowered employees are more likely to take initiative, and as the example of the USS Santa Fe shows, this leads to a more proactive and resilient workforce.

It is often unseen and unrecognised, but when a creative problem-solving approach is shared by many, it fulfils the role of a shared language that helps bridge gaps between departments and hierarchies. It facilitates crisper and clearer communication as everyone understands the stages of where everybody else is at, and clarifies the rules of engagement. This common ground reduces misunderstandings and ensures that all team members can quickly align around a common goal. Highly effective teams all share a common language that acts like "shorthand" for getting things done, and a creative problem-solving approach is the DNA of shared language.

For an SLT to successfully integrate a creative problem-solving approach into an organisation, it is best not to label it as such. As soon as you give an approach such a label, you are sure to turn people off. Rather, just talk about "our way of working" and structure questions and any supporting materials under three headings that suit the mood of the environment (e.g. understand the problem, generate ideas, plan for action, etc).

Key factors for success in seeding such a framework in a business are:

Leadership commitment, where leaders champion the adoption of the methodology and demonstrate its value through conversations, decision-making and actions. Adopting the simple language in a disciplined way and leading by example sets the tone for the rest of the organisation.

Training and development to provide comprehensive training to ensure all employees understand and can effectively apply "our way of working." Make full use of online resources and any related videos to help embed core concepts and continue to reinforce them. Continuous improvement helps to keep the application of such an innovative approach relevant.

Tailor the chosen approach and its language to fit the organisation's unique culture and needs, and provide some worked examples. This customisation ensures relevance and increases the likelihood of successful adoption. To that end, framing conversations using Marquet's Ladder of Leadership is helpful.

The role of a leader is not simply to solve the problem, but to step in where leadership is most needed. Often, this means helping the team frame the problem by clarifying what's really at stake and what needs to be addressed. As the team deepens its understanding, new information may emerge that challenges the original framing. In these moments, effective leadership means listening carefully and being willing to revisit and reframe the problem so the team stays focused on what truly matters.

Recognition and reward employees who effectively use the "our way of working" to solve real issues and problems and make sustainable improvements. This recognition reinforces desired behaviours and encourages others to follow.

Regularly assess and refine "our way of working" to ensure it keeps pace with any changing dynamics.

Appreciative Inquiry is one example of a creative problem-solving approach that focuses on identifying and leveraging an organisation's strengths. By asking questions like "What are we doing well?" and "How can we build on these successes?", Appreciative Inquiry sets a "can-do, will-do" climate for problem-solving. This approach, subtle and unnoticed as it may seem, has also been proven to promote employee engagement and drive transformational change by focusing on possibilities rather than deficiencies.

I had the very good fortune a few years ago of working with the senior team of one of the largest organisations on the planet, employing over 120,000 people. The business was struggling to adapt to the impact of the 2007 "credit crunch" and bounce back in a cost-efficient manner. We went around the room to complete introductions. I was struck by the experiences shared as each individual touched on past roles in locations around the globe, across different functions and how they each faced the challenges of driving growth in unique cultures in other languages.

However, in the room, there was also a unifying common language that was used to diagnose and break down problems, set goals, figure out solutions, plan a response and prepare people and material for execution. It was a language comprised of "company slang" and some gestures used to make decisions "on the fly." They impressed as they were deeply ingrained in the organisation and focused on what needed to be done to move forward. A rigorous approach built on creative problem-solving was at the heart of the common language, and it was deployed with full force and to great effect.

The most inspiring aspect of leadership is creating more leaders, not more followers. Establishing a common language and standardised ways of working within an organisation is pivotal for cultivating leadership at all levels and transforming traditional followers into proactive leaders. A shared framework, embedded in the culture and ways of working, ensures clarity in communication, reduces misunderstandings and aligns team members around common objectives.

When everyone operates with the same terminology and processes, it fosters a cohesive environment where individuals feel confident to take the initiative. Such an environment not only streamlines work patterns to create value but also empowers employees to make informed decisions and builds leadership capabilities. The approach is rooted in empowerment, promoting a culture where leadership is a collective responsibility that drives innovation and organisational success.

Summary

Psychological safety is the foundation of high-performing teams. It gives people permission to speak up, challenge assumptions and speak truth to power without fear of blame or retribution. In SLTs where the stakes are high and egos can be fragile, creating this safety is critical to unlocking honest dialogue, innovation and effective decision-making.

Giving feedback to a CEO about a failing business strategy is one of the most delicate challenges anybody can face. It requires a balance of courage, respect and clarity. Arguably, the most effective way to approach it is not as a confrontation, but as a contribution to the shared goal of organisational success. Rather than delivering a verdict, it's better to invite dialogue. Open questions, such as "How do you interpret these results?" or "Could we be missing something?" allow a CEO space to reflect and engage. With respect, timing and the right tone, difficult feedback can become the catalyst for a meaningful course correction and a stronger, more resilient leadership dialogue, with multiple heads shaping and steering the organisation instead of just one.

Intentional leadership, as exemplified by David Marquet in *Turn the Ship Around*, reinforces this environment by shifting authority to where the information resides. His "Ladder of Leadership" approach empowers individuals to move from "Tell me what to do" to "Here's what I intend to do," fostering ownership, accountability and initiative across the team. Above all, it fosters an enactive development process that treats strategy as a living, evolving response to the realities a team discovers through action. Organisations learn by doing, by testing assumptions, sensing feedback and adapting in real-time. The intentional leadership approach empowers teams to co-create strategy as they engage with the world, making it more resilient, responsive and relevant. Rather than waiting for certainty, an enactive strategy embraces uncertainty as fuel for insight and innovation, encouraging teams to "boldly go."

When this is combined with creative problem-solving techniques such as reframing issues or generating non-obvious options, SLTs become even more agile in addressing complex challenges. Establishing a shared language and structured approach to resolving issues further strengthens clarity and cohesion. For SLTs, this not only accelerates decision-making and builds trust but also shapes a collective leadership identity grounded in intentional action, openness and shared responsibility.

Reflective Questions

The questions set out below are designed to help you internalise key ideas, examine your own experiences in light of what you've read and consider how any insights might shape your thinking and actions in future. There are no right answers, only honest ones. Use these opportunities to reflect, to deepen your awareness, spark conversation with others or simply increase awareness of what's changing for you as you make progress through this book.

> Are our expectations and desired outcomes clearly communicated when delegating tasks? Do we lead with intent? Do we stop to ask what others recommend we do?

> Do our managers know what "empowerment" looks like in action? Have we equipped them to lead that way?

> How do we rate at giving feedback? When we ask for feedback, does accountability silently shift back to resting on our shoulders?

> What common language or framework could unite teams across functions and levels when facing complex challenges?

There is a longer list of questions in the "Appendix: Reflective Questions." These are designed to be addressed when you, with or without the team, have more time available for reflection, rather than reaction.

Chapter 5
Set Up for Success

"We shape our buildings, and afterwards our buildings shape us."
– Winston Churchill, Statesman

Structure is one of the most powerful and often overlooked levers available to senior leadership teams (SLTs). While strategy defines direction, it is structure that enables execution by shaping how people collaborate, make decisions and move resources across the business. Yet, in many organisations, structure becomes an afterthought – a set of boxes and lines on a page that reflects past compromises rather than future ambitions. This chapter challenges that default and invites SLTs to take a fresh, deliberate look at how structure underpins performance.

When done well, organisational structure is more than a chart; it's a blueprint for value creation.[1] It ensures that roles are clear, decision rights are understood and work flows seamlessly to the teams best positioned to deliver. But when left untended, structure can drift, becoming bloated, misaligned or quietly political. It can hinder accountability, slow decision-making and trap talent in the wrong places. Through practical examples and hard-won lessons, this chapter shows how to diagnose structural friction and redesign for clarity, agility and scale.

At the heart of this work is a mindset shift: from treating structure as a static artefact to seeing it as a living part of the business's operating system. You will explore how to align form with function, match people to purpose and embed systems that balance control with flexibility. You will also be introduced to frameworks, such as the Burke-Litwin model, that help leadership teams understand how structure interacts with culture, leadership and performance. Because when structure serves strategy and people – not the other way around – everything gets easier.

A Place for Everything, Everything in Its Place

Organisational structure is the backbone of any business. However, in many cases, businesses end up with two very different versions: the formal structure found on outdated organisational charts and the informal structure of how people actually work together to get things done. When these two diverge, confusion sets in. While organisation structure is not the whole story of how a business operates, it is a crucial part of how strategy is delivered and work gets managed.

It's the job of the SLT to shape and maintain a structure that works. That means putting the right people in the right roles, aligning responsibilities with how work flows and ensuring decisions can be made quickly and clearly. But over time, structures often drift – adjusted again and again to fit short-term fixes or built around strong personalities who find ways to work around the gaps. The result? Inefficiencies, bottlenecks and a structure that feels anything but agile or affordable.

Some say no organisation structure should go unchallenged for more than two years. That might be ambitious, but regular reviews are wise, especially if they focus on what really matters: how work gets done and value is created. It's tempting to launch big structural overhauls, but often, more minor changes to workflows and responsibilities can deliver better results with less disruption. In one service business I worked with, a sprawling international structure had outgrown the demand it was built for. By reassigning roles based on actual work activities, they ended up with a leaner, more effective structure that truly served their customers.

At its core, an organisation's structure sets out how work is coordinated and who holds what authority. After decades of working with companies, it still surprises me how few have a clear, up-to-date view of their organisational structure, along with an accompanying record of delegated authority. More often, I see a few names in boxes, mismatched titles and some hastily added dotted lines during an explanation. This matters because headcount and its associated costs regularly make up the single largest charge on the profit and loss account, yet the design process by which headcount is directed and managed bears little relationship to its value.

The language we use to describe structure can be equally messy. Terms get misused, become mangled and often mean different things to different people. That is why shared language and mental models are so important. High-performing organisations speak the same language when it comes to how work and structure interact.

In fast-growing businesses, I often hear leaders describe their structure as a "network" or "a living force" that resists being captured in a 2D chart. That sounds exciting, but in practice, it can lead to a lack of clarity, job insecurity and unclear career paths. The structure, meant to reflect agility, ends up creating ambiguity. Quite simply, the organisation structure that such leaders describe actually describes very little of substance, leaving open a void that is subsequently filled with questions and (wild) interpretation. The organisational structure cited as evidence to express a business's operating architecture falls uncomfortably short. Charts do not need to show everything, but they should show something that is clear and consistent. Clear is kind. Unclear is unkind.[2]

Organisation charts serve a specific purpose: they show reporting lines, decision rights and role placement for planning and accountability. They are not designed to show how every task gets done.[3] For that, we need other models, maps and workflows. But even these can only work if there's a shared understanding of process and control. Organisation design is about striking a balance between how work gets done (process) and how it's governed (control). Good processes make workflow. They reduce duplication, speed up decisions and support scaling. But without control, things get messy. Without process, things stall. The best structures allow both to work in harmony, creating consistent, high-quality outcomes.

The SLT is ultimately responsible for shaping this operating system. There are four core areas where deliberate design matters most:

1. Structural Design

The SLT defines strategic goals and ensures they are embedded in operational processes. The overarching design principles that guide organisational form and shape – whether the business adopts a functional, team, process, divisional or matrix-based structure (see graphic below) – are a deliberate choice. These choices are informed by "systems thinking" that maps out key influences and dynamics.

Challenges such as strategy alignment, talent matching, scalability, operational complexity, affordability and the need for flexibility are assessed when developing a structural design.

Build a mix of "hard and soft" performance metrics and governance frameworks to review the effectiveness of the organisation's structure.

Think of the business as a value delivery system, not just a cost centre. To do so requires data insight that shows how value is added and helps illustrate how value can be maximised.

2. Delegation and Hierarchy

Create a simple and clear definition of layers and spans, illustrating reporting lines and chains of command.

Establish decision-making authority at different levels throughout the organisation to ensure agility without compromising control.

The SLT is aware of its leadership philosophy and how the SLT's behaviours influence outcomes along the spectrum of centralised decision-making (top-down command and control) to decentralised and empowered decision-making (distributed authority). The leadership philosophy is mirrored within the structure.

3. Workforce Deployment

This is how work departments are structured and how resources are allocated.

The shape and size of specialised teams to ensure quality, cost and regulatory compliance, and what is required to sustain efficiency and innovation

The balance of permanent staff and contract staff required for the work involves striking a balance between flexibility and stability, skill availability and development, company culture and fulfilling business growth forecasts.

4. Managing Change

This includes how business process re-engineering, lean management initiatives and digital transformation efforts are sponsored and directed. It also extends to how organisational units evolve through mergers and acquisitions, and how they respond to significant shifts in customer behaviour and technological innovation – such as the adoption of AI, which drives automation, role redesign and, in some cases, redundancy.

Workforce expectations are also shifting. Employees now seek greater flexibility and more meaningful career development. Static structures and outdated policies risk losing top talent to more agile and responsive organisations.

Leadership development programmes are essential for building a strong internal talent pipeline, enabling effective succession planning – rather than relying solely on deputies or assistants listed on an organisation chart.

Organisation structure may not be glamorous, but it is powerful. When done well, it delivers clarity, speed and performance. Done poorly, it drags on progress. The best senior leadership teams treat it as a strategic asset – one that aligns people, purpose and process to drive results.

Alternative Organisation Structure Models

Defining organisational design principles helps bring the company's vision, values and strategic goals to life before drafting an organisational structure. Clarifying organisational design principles and ensuring their execution is a core role of the SLT. Without leadership promoting clear design principles, the organisation's structure risks evolving in a fragmented way, resulting in inefficiencies, misaligned priorities, wasted time, effort and confusion. The cost-effectiveness of a business is frequently a function of its organisational structure. Design principles often include such considerations as:

- Be "flat" and move decision-making to the lowest practicable safe level.

- Keep the corporate centre small (e.g. for functions such as HR and Finance)

- No more than five management layers operating with an average span of control of eight

- Build processes to solve customer problems and outsource everything else

Such design considerations are helpful but secondary to determining the most appropriate organisational shape and form, such as the six options shown below, which reflect work dynamics.

Process

If business drivers require
- Short cycle times
- Close control

Team based

If business drivers require
- Highly integrated work
- Work that can be grouped around definitive outcomes
- Focused effort to produce a collective outcome

Functional

| Functional Expertise A | Functional Expertise B | Functional Expertise C | Functional Expertise D |

If business drivers require
- Specialised skills
- Specialist functions serving multiple customers
- Delivery of diverse complex products

Matrix

Function 1   Function 2   Function 3

Customer A
Customer B
Customer C

If business drivers require:
- Substantial project working
- Mobilisation of multi-skilled teams while maintaining functional expertise

Geographical/Market/Customer

| Geography/ Market/ Customer 1 | Geography/ Market/ Customer 2 | Geography/ Market/ Customer 3 |

Functional expertise
If business drivers require:
- Sensitivity and rapid response to local needs

Product

| Product Group 1 | Product Group 2 | Product Group 2 |

Functional expertise
If business drivers require:
- Rapid product development

1. Functional Structure

Employees are grouped within specialised functions such as marketing, finance, operations and human resources. Each function operates under the leadership of a functional head.

Advantages:

- Specialisation enhances expertise and efficiency and provides clear lines of authority

- Robust skill development and clear career progression within each function

- Decision-making within functions results in operational consistency

Disadvantages:

- Functional structures can lead to silos, which hamper collaboration

- Sluggish and slow decision-making due to hierarchical approval processes

- Lower flexibility in responding to external market changes

Functional structures are best suited to stable organisations with specialised departments and clear hierarchies. This is where operational efficiency is a primary focus, such as in large corporations or government agencies. However, functions may also be the first organising principle of a rapidly developing business, where they can facilitate early scale-up phases when adding and attracting talent before more complex business operations evolve.

2. Team Structure

Employees work in cross-functional teams that are empowered to make decisions. The culture of such businesses typically emphasises collaboration (over hierarchy), customer and purpose-driven empowerment, shared responsibility, continuous learning and adaptability.

Advantages:

- Faster decision-making within units: value streams, products or customer segments

- Enhanced employee engagement and empowerment

- High levels of innovation and flexibility

Disadvantages:

- Risks of role ambiguity and conflict due to a lack of formal hierarchy

- Can be inefficient if coordination between teams is weak

- Requires strong leadership to align teams with strategic goals

Team-based structures are ideal for dynamic and innovative environments where transparent, frequent communication is required and effective collaboration, agility and problem-solving are crucial.

Such structures are common in tech startups and research-driven companies, where a growth mindset is encouraged across all levels, and individuals are expected to self-manage and contribute beyond their narrow job descriptions.

3. Process

Employees are organised around core business processes (e.g. order fulfilment, customer service) where the focus is on speed and workflow efficiency when handling well-defined products or standardised services.

Advantages:

- Optimises efficiency and customer satisfaction
- Reduces bottlenecks by streamlining processes
- Institutionalises multi-skilled collaboration

Disadvantages:

- Problematic to implement in traditional hierarchical organisations
- Requires continuous optimisation and monitoring
- Employees may struggle with role ambiguity

Process-based structures are most suitable for businesses or organisational units focused on optimising workflows and efficiency, particularly in industries such as manufacturing, logistics and service operations.

4. Product-Based Structure

The organisation is divided into semi-autonomous units based on product lines. Each division has its own resources and management.

Advantages:

- Enhances responsiveness to market needs and regional demands

- Enables accountability and ownership at an operating divisional level vs corporate

- Encourages entrepreneurial thinking and action within divisions

Disadvantages:

- Duplication of resources across divisions increases costs

- Potential conflicts will likely arise between the corporate centre and divisions

- Presents challenges to building a unified corporate culture that promotes movement

Divisional structures are well-suited for companies with multiple and distinct product lines, which require different strategies, skills and operations that a more dedicated focus can provide, primarily when serving different customer groups. Divisions are found in multinational consumer goods, large-scale financial services and international technology firms when the company becomes too large or complex for a single functional strategy to be effective. Divisions are also suitable for businesses that have diversified through acquisition and now operate distinct companies, where it's beneficial to measure and manage each division as a separate entity under one umbrella.

5. Market-Based Structure

The business is structured around customer segments, industries or geographic regions to better serve specific market needs.

Advantages:

- A customer-centric approach enhances responsiveness

- Adapts well to diverse markets and regional demands

- Enables specialisation in market trends and customer behaviours

Disadvantages:

- Risks of resource duplication across different markets

- Adds complexity when coordinating management initiatives across market segments

- Can be costly due to decentralised operations

Market-based structures are most suitable for organisations operating in multiple regions, industries or customer segments, such as global retail chains or operating within different regulatory regimes, such as for financial services firms.

6. Matrix Structure

Employees report to both a functional manager and a project task manager, creating a dual-command system.

Advantages:

- Encourages knowledge sharing and collaboration across skill groups

- Enhances flexibility in responding to dynamic market needs

- Optimises resource utilisation by leveraging cross-functional teams

Disadvantages:

- Can lead to confusion and conflicts over reporting relationships

- Demands effort to set objectives, manage feedback and evaluate performance

- Risk of power struggles between functional and project managers

The matrix structure is considered a pragmatic approach for complex organisations that require both functional expertise and project-based collaboration (e.g. multinational corporations and consulting firms). However, the matrix structure requires careful application, as it can become a hotbed of confusion, stress and frustration as individuals struggle to balance and trade off multiple demands and priorities. Functional and project leaders are prone to competing for resources, influence and control, and inter-unit tension can result in political behaviour that hinders effective decision-making. A matrix works well when there's strong collaboration, clear communication and mutual respect across reporting lines. In low-trust cultures, it can quickly break down into conflict and inaction.

Challenges of Operating Within Structure

Many new members to an SLT rightly celebrate their appointment as a crowning moment of their career. For many new appointments, it takes time for the gravity of the role, the scope of leadership responsibilities and the understanding of capability requirements to truly sink in. It is an enlightened MD that prompts reflection by SLT leaders on how they can contribute to business topics about which SLT leaders have had little or no preparation. As one SLT leader put it, "I came to realise that I may have a hand on the steering wheel, but I have not had lessons on how to drive!"

The influence of the SLT on organisation structure cannot be overstated. Yet, it seems many sleepwalk their way through the subject and passively accept what exists, if only because there is a comfort in the structure that provided a SLT leader's point of entry to the business and/or their ascent "to the top."

When it comes to reviewing organisation structures, SLTs are often stymied by four forces that operate both within and outside the boundaries of their business:

1. Power Struggles and Internal Politics

Different leaders and departments can have conflicting interests regarding a chosen structure. In a functional structure, where functions operate independently, function heads often resist changes that reduce their authority and autonomy. Conversely, in a matrix structure, which involves shared responsibilities across multiple teams, conflicts can arise over decision-making power. Reconciling these power dynamics requires clarity of purpose as well as mature communication skills to ensure that the chosen structure serves the business rather than an individual SLT leader's agenda in the pursuit of power.

Patrick Lencioni, author of *Five Dysfunctions of a Team*,[4] offers a direct question to help flush out what often lies behind conflict: "What is your first team?" Suppose the answer that comes back is the direct teams that SLT leaders lead, rather than prioritising their fellow SLT leaders. In that case, the result is unwinnable, drawn-out conflicts that handicap the business's progress and development. For the avoidance of any doubt, direct reports are "second teams."

2. Resistance to Change

Organisation restructuring often faces resistance from employees at multiple levels within a business, particularly middle managers, who may feel – with some justification – that their position has come under threat, if not wholly compromised. SLTs should navigate resistance carefully, as poorly handled restructuring activities lead to demotivation, loss of key talent and reduced productivity.

The power challenges that emerge when existing teams or individuals feel they are losing influence due to structural changes often result in hidden opposition and, in extreme cases, overt efforts to sabotage a proposed transition. By contrast, SLTs tend to view restructuring as a technical activity. In reality, it's deeply political and emotional, with covert resistance commonly operating under the guise of "practical concerns" and a ripple effect that goes far and wide. One should not underestimate the capacity of experienced managers to use their knowledge and credibility to stall change.

Niccolò Machiavelli put it eloquently: "There is nothing more difficult to take in hand, more perilous to conduct, or more uncertain in its success, than to take the lead in the introduction of a new order of things."[5]

3. Social and Cultural Expectations

Political pressures can also be prompted by shifting expectations that emerge in a changing society. Businesses are under increasing scrutiny to adopt inclusive structures and ensure diversity in leadership and decision-making, rather than structures based solely on "merit." Hierarchical structures with little or low representation of women or minority groups frequently attract negative attention and can damage a company's reputation.

To reflect these broader societal shifts, SLTs should consider reshaping leadership roles, reporting structures and workforce strategies to foster greater inclusion. Embracing a wider range of lived and learned experiences enriches decision-making, strengthens team dynamics and brings fresh insight to the challenges and opportunities every organisation faces.

4. Organisational Agility vs Bureaucracy

As the pace of economic and business change accelerates, balancing agility with the necessary processes and controls that ensure quality outcomes comes under increasing pressure. Making a company more agile can be politically risky, as it may threaten traditional power hierarchies and create friction between SLT leaders and their respective management teams, who may see benefits for themselves in a more rigid system.

Office politics and "power plays" among senior directors often stem from a combination of interpersonal and psychological factors. Organisational structure can also be a factor, with competition over limited budgets and resources, as well as over poorly defined and/or ambiguous roles. "Politics" and "power plays," if they are allowed to flourish, can seriously distract SLT leaders.

Understanding the Burke-Litwin Model

The Burke-Litwin model[6] of organisational performance offers an illuminating perspective on understanding how different elements within an overall organisation interact and how senior leadership can shape and influence outcomes. The model can form part of a team-based approach to understanding and aligning different elements of an organisation's operating architecture to drive performance and achieve strategic goals.

The Burke-Litwin model sets out twelve interdependent factors that affect an organisation's performance, which are grouped into three categories:

1. **Transformational factors** or fundamental, deep-seated elements that drive major change

2. **Transactional factors** or operational and procedural aspects that influence performance

3. **Individual and performance factors** or personal attributes and behaviours that affect results

Each of these factors plays a role in shaping the organisational culture, engagement and overall effectiveness, and provides a map by which the SLT can steer the collective organisation and design interventions to effect positive change.

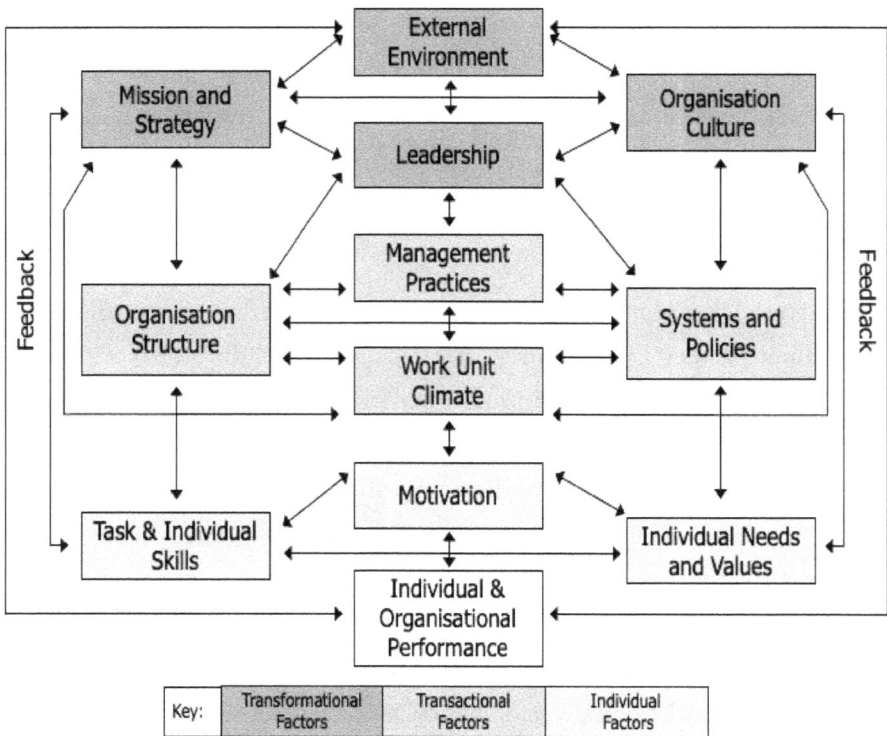

Applying the Burke-Litwin Model

Transformational Factors (Deep Change Drivers)

External environment. A role of the SLT is to proactively scan for market trends, regulatory changes and competitive pressures. By sharing and integrating external insights, SLT leaders ensure that the operating business model is well-matched to counter external challenges and take advantage of opportunities.

Leadership. "Strong leadership" fosters a healthy work environment, and for "strong leadership" to thrive, the SLT models the behaviours that align with corporate values to shape a positive and healthy work culture. Leadership coaching and moderated 360-degree feedback can help leaders refine their effectiveness and performance.

Mission and strategy. A well-defined mission provides purpose, while a clear strategy helps ensure alignment with detailed action plans. The SLT's role is to consistently communicate strategy, helping employees understand how their roles and work contribute to the organisation's strategic long-term goals.

Organisational culture. A high-performing organisation thrives on a culture of trust, accountability and innovation. The SLT actively shapes and reinforces desired cultural norms through values-based leadership, recognition programmes and frequent two-way communication to achieve business objectives.

Transactional Factors (Operational Performance Drivers)

Structure. The SLT ensures that the optimum organisational structure supports collaboration rather than silos, enhances efficiency and makes clear accountability.

Systems and policies. Performance management, decision-making frameworks and HR policies are designed to reinforce productivity and support resource utilisation. Streamlining processes reduces bureaucracy and empowers employees to be more effective.

Work unit climate. The SLT fosters an environment of psychological safety, where employees feel valued and heard, and conflict is proactively identified, handled and resolved. Regular pulse surveys and "Town Halls" can improve communication and engagement.

Management practices. Middle managers play a key role in execution. Leadership development programmes can help managers adopt coaching-based leadership styles that drive team performance and encourage continuous improvement.

Task and individual skills. The SLT ensures that employees are deployed in roles that align with their strengths, thereby enhancing productivity and job satisfaction.

Individual and Performance Factors

Motivation. People perform best when they are motivated. The SLT ensures that reward and recognition programmes go beyond compensation and address intrinsic motivators, such as purpose-driven work and career growth opportunities.

Individual needs and values. Understanding employee aspirations and aligning them with organisational objectives builds loyalty and commitment. The SLT ensures the performance management highlights development needs, and action is taken to fulfil these needs.

Individual and organisational performance. The ultimate goal is sustained high performance. The SLT continuously measure progress using KPIs, scorecards, employee feedback and performance analytics to refine strategies and implement improvement plans.

The SLT plays a crucial role in shaping, managing and improving an organisation's operating architecture, functioning and operations. Profiling the business using the Burke-Litwin model helps identify gaps, missed opportunities and sparks a more comprehensive approach to addressing organisational needs.

Organisation structure is a fundamental determinant of business success, and the attention it frequently receives falls between two stools. It is either underpowered and underestimated, or it is seen as the "final solution" to many of the ills besetting an organisation, when alternative, less disruptive solutions can be introduced.

Structures define how work is coordinated, how decisions are made and how efficiently resources are utilised. Different models – functional, divisional, matrix, flat and network structures – offer unique advantages and challenges depending on an organisation's objectives and value proposition. However, no structure should remain static nor be left unattended. Organisations that continuously assess and refine their structure and resourcing strategies are best positioned to achieve long-term success.

Summary

Choosing the right organisational structure is a critical enabler of successful strategy execution. The structure must support how value is created and delivered, whether that's achieved by structures that emphasise functional excellence, cross-functional teams, operating and deploying to end-to-end business processes, products, market sectors or a matrix-led structure. Structure itself should never be the starting point. Clarity on design principles, such as affordability, agility, accountability, customer focus and speed of decision-making, must come first to ensure the structure serves the strategy, not the other way around.

While structure provides the formal scaffolding for strategy execution, it is the human experience within that structure that ultimately drives performance. A well-designed organisation not only enables clarity, speed and accountability, but it also fosters a sense of belonging, autonomy and purpose. Chapter 3 has shown that when people feel heard, supported and empowered in their roles, happiness rises and with it, productivity. Structure alone doesn't deliver results; it's how people feel and function within it that determines whether the strategy truly comes to life.

Structure can create challenges. Internal politics, resistance to change and layers of bureaucracy often emerge when structures are misaligned or poorly understood. This is why tools like the Burke-Litwin model are so useful: They help leaders assess organisational effectiveness holistically, showing how structure interacts with leadership, culture, systems and employee motivations. Understanding how an organisation's inner workings affect structure, and how these can change over time, helps senior leaders design and adapt structures that actually work. Put simply, when structure aligns with the business's operations, it helps to drive better performance and supports long-term growth.

Reflective Questions

The questions set out below are designed to help you internalise key ideas, examine your own experiences in light of what you've read and consider how any insights might shape your thinking and actions in future. There are no right answers, only honest ones. Use these opportunities to reflect, to deepen your awareness, spark conversation with others or simply increase awareness of what's changing for you as you make progress through this book.

Are the most strategically important parts of the business positioned with the right influence, visibility and resources?

Where do we experience delays or bottlenecks due to the way we're organised?

Are we maximising the talent we have, or is it being underutilised in the wrong part of the organisation?

Where do we see confusion, conflict or misalignment between teams?

Where are we already seeing signals that the structure is becoming a constraint?

There is a longer list of questions in the "Appendix: Reflective Questions." These are designed to be addressed when you, with or without the team, have more time available for reflection, rather than reaction.

Chapter 6
Strategy for Execution

"Vision without execution is hallucination.
Execution without strategy is a nightmare"
– Japanese proverb

It's one thing to write a business strategy; it's another to actually make it happen. Too often, the most well-intentioned strategies fail not because the ideas were weak but because they were never wholly owned, understood or executed. This chapter examines the persistent gap between strategy and delivery, highlighting the importance of senior leadership team (SLT) involvement in bridging it. Strategy, when done right, becomes more than a set of statements – it becomes a shared commitment to a bold and achievable future.

Drawing on real-world experiences, this chapter unpacks common traps that derail even the most promising plans, such as building a strategy purely to raise finance, relying on the MD's vision without broader SLT buy-in or failing to adapt when circumstances change. It introduces a practical and inclusive approach to building a strategy blueprint – a clear, structured plan that aligns vision, goals, actions and ownership. The focus here is not on big ideas alone but on embedding strategy into everyday decisions, conversations and behaviours.

Central to this process is the role of constructive conflict. High-performing SLTs do not avoid disagreement – they embrace it.

Developing a strategy that the whole team is committed to often means surfacing tough questions, challenging assumptions and working through tensions. This kind of purposeful friction isn't a sign of dysfunction but of maturity. It ensures that the strategy is tested from multiple angles, shaped by diverse perspectives and grounded in operational reality. Without honest back-and-forth, strategies risk becoming vague statements of intent rather than actionable, resilient plans. Commitment doesn't come from consensus at any cost – it comes from feeling heard, respected and involved in the hard graft of shaping the future together.

This chapter walks through five key phases of creating a strategy blueprint, each designed to bring clarity, alignment and accountability to the process. From understanding where the business stands today to mapping out strategic options, building consensus and turning plans into action, this is a roadmap for transforming strategy from a document into a dynamic force for progress. The goal is not just a good strategy on paper, but excellent execution in practice, led and owned by the very team that created it.

This chapter should be read together with Chapter 7, which outlines the application of a management execution system to drive the expected results from the strategy that is created, developed and planned.

Strategy Shapes the Future

A clear strategy is the backbone of any successful business. Strategy has the special ability to provide direction, align the organisation around shared goals and ensure that resources are focused on what matters most. If there is no clear strategy, even the most talented teams become diverted and pulled in different directions. A well-defined strategy not only clarifies what the business aims to achieve but also outlines how it will succeed, helping leaders make better decisions, adapt to change and stay ahead of the competition. It's the difference between simply reacting to circumstances and actively shaping the future.

However, in my conversations with business leaders, it is rare not to learn about how even the best-laid plans fail to deliver results. The various descriptions of how "the best" plans unravel are always revealing to listen to. Often, I hear business leaders candidly confess the following shortcomings:

Weak Understanding of Target Market and What Drives Value

There was a weak understanding of the target customers' needs that drive value and the shifts in market dynamics that signal emerging opportunities. As a result, the plans created lack genuine clarity. What the business stands for, what makes it distinctive and why customers should buy what is offered is not fully profiled, understood and documented.

To add further distraction, "off-the-shelf" business reporting systems encourage managing on averages rather than spotlighting the best that can be done in the business. Deeper analysis is required, which extends beyond tracking the average, to reveal where and how value is created internally and which activities constitute waste. There are immediate benefits from reallocating resources away from the loss-making areas towards those of high profitability. Understanding why certain products, customers or channels are unusually profitable or unprofitable provides invaluable factual insights for future development.

The key learning is to take a step back and adopt a clear-headed approach – to truly understand the business as if its various parts comprise a system for delivering value – and then design the reporting systems so that they can be managed to optimise delivery.

The Business Plan is Built to Raise Finance

What actually exists is a plan for raising finance, not one for growing and running a business. The numbers invariably add up to an attractive investment opportunity, which lulls the reader into a false sense of security and overconfidence. However, investors and banks do not make strategy happen – management does. The primary role and function of an SLT is to create and execute a viable, sustainable business strategy.

Finance-led plans, even if realistic, often fail to connect the dots and frequently lack clear specifications of the management actions required to deliver the strategy. These plans do not help employees get on board or feel excited by the vision and goals. They are distinguished by a vacuum, as there has been little or no thinking about what the business's strategy actually is or how it will be sustained. As a result, any strategic thinking that does happen is done "on the fly" under pressure. In that context, it quickly becomes a tactical decision-making process, and the clarity of purpose around a vision and its related mission is lost. So, at the end of the day, something is actioned and delivered – but it's not what was in the plan, because nothing much existed.

Overtaken By Events

The strategy that is developed is overtaken by events. The planning process employed does not keep pace with market changes. As the gap widens between what is actually happening and what was intended, a belief emerges that developing a plan is a pointless waste of time. Any plans that do exist are fixed in time, inflexible and not updated.

Events happen – COVID-19, the war in Ukraine, Donald Trump, new market entrants, a sudden price drop or the loss of key talent – and it is imperative that there is a plan B in place for how to adapt. If it's the only thing I learned from some of the world's largest companies, it is that when a crunch moment comes, they are prepared. They have plans B, C and D, with strategies primed and ready to deploy when the cycle turns. Priority work continues; the core mission is still delivered, customers are supported and the focus on how and when is restructured at speed to address creative problem-solving. To be nimble requires planning, not just an entrepreneurial mindset.

Given how frequently external changes occur and how far-reaching their impact can be, leadership teams should create risk-based plans that incorporate options – so when the "tide that lifts all boats goes out," they can act swiftly on well-considered decisions.

The MD's Plan

It was the MD's plan. All too often, the MD produces the plan, but nobody on the SLT is emotionally connected with what the plan intends to deliver or how its execution is managed. Clever and smart the plan may be, but it's one person's plan – and nobody else's. Sadly, the life of this type of plan is very short, as it receives little attention.

An unfortunate and all-too-common dynamic is sparked when the gap between the performance achieved and what was outlined in the plan grows. Accountability for the plan's delivery is seen as belonging solely to the MD, who now faces the added challenge of trying to win over SLT support for a plan that is seen as failing.

Strategy Is Not Embedded in Management Conversations

All too often, business planning is seen as a one-off annual exercise to set a budget and is divorced from regular management meetings. The strategy "away day" at a fine country house hotel yields some stimulating and healthy exchanges, as well as fostering positive and fresh thinking. But at best, it creates a "conspiracy of optimism" where everybody who has "talked it out" then thinks it's all set fair. Action planning is conspicuous by its absence.

Ken Blanchard is an influential author, best known for his "One Minute Manager" book series and his work on situational leadership with Paul Hersey. The Ken Blanchard Organisation[1] surveyed 700 businesses, seeking to understand why strategies fail in delivery, and neatly summarised the key findings below:

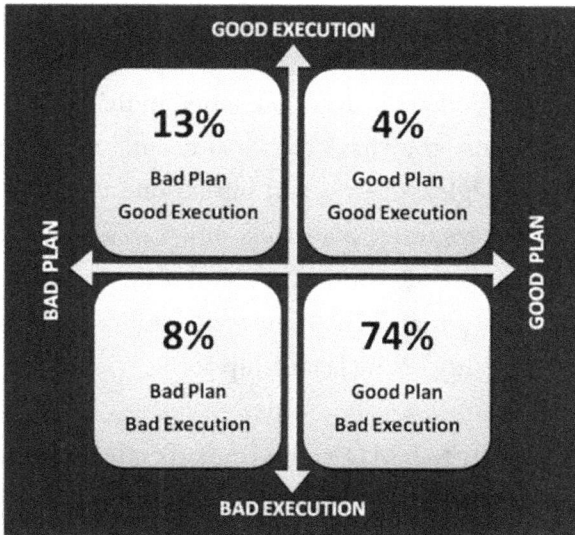

Nobody will disagree that a clearly articulated and well-executed strategy is essential for success. Yet, the yawning gap between strategic intent and operational reality remains a common challenge for many companies. At the heart of bridging this gap is the active involvement of the SLT in developing a comprehensive strategy blueprint.

A well-structured and coherent strategy blueprint serves as a guide for the business, ensuring that every function and employee is aligned with the business's vision and goals.

In every debate about "what is our strategy here?", it is imperative that the MD stimulates discussions on the issues that drive progress towards achieving the "main quest" and avoids "side quests" that generate low impact.

Businesses often fall short of their goals because the top team is not aligned on "the most important things to do that matter" and is not working together, instead pursuing individual "side quests." Often, this is because they have not "had it out," and the debate that needs to happen is glossed over and buried due to a fear of conflict. Consequently, any resulting plan lacks traction and commitment in the work practices and behaviours that bind teams together. Managing conflict is a key test for an MD. How well conflict is resolved is a key indicator of the quality of the leadership team.

To engage the SLT, the MD should not dictate what others think but lead with questions that surface divergent perspectives, creating an empowered, action-oriented work environment founded on intentional leadership. Brainstorming can be fun, but at this level, it can also seem messy and time-consuming. To help bring about the necessary convergence, the MD should think "FAB" to help the SLT produce a strategy blueprint:

> **Focus** and make finding and staying with the right direction the "main quest."

> **Align** and ensure the SLT engages in constructive, respectful and philosophically healthy debate about the business that avoids taking swipes at each other and absent colleagues.

> **Benefits** or identify the work activity that adds value and prioritise it.

A robust strategy blueprint encompasses key elements, including the company's vision, values, mission, value proposition, three-year strategic goals, key strategies for achieving those goals, operating structure, KPIs, financial plan and budgets, and a detailed implementation plan. Central to the implementation plan is the establishment of annual goals and the use of a management execution system, such as OKRs (detailed in Chapter 7), to measure and drive progress, as well as hold teams and individuals accountable.

The 5 Phases of SLT Engagement in Creating the Strategy Blueprint

Producing a strategy blueprint is not a one-off event but a phased and iterative process. It requires the SLT to collaborate deeply, challenge assumptions and ultimately come together with a clarity of purpose around a common destination and shared path forward. By integrating the management processes used to execute an implementation plan, the strategy blueprint provides the roadmap for translating strategy into action. The foundations of a "good plan" and "good execution" are in place.

This process of engagement with the SLT unfolds over five key phases – in marked contrast to the conventional wisdom of a single "strategy away day":

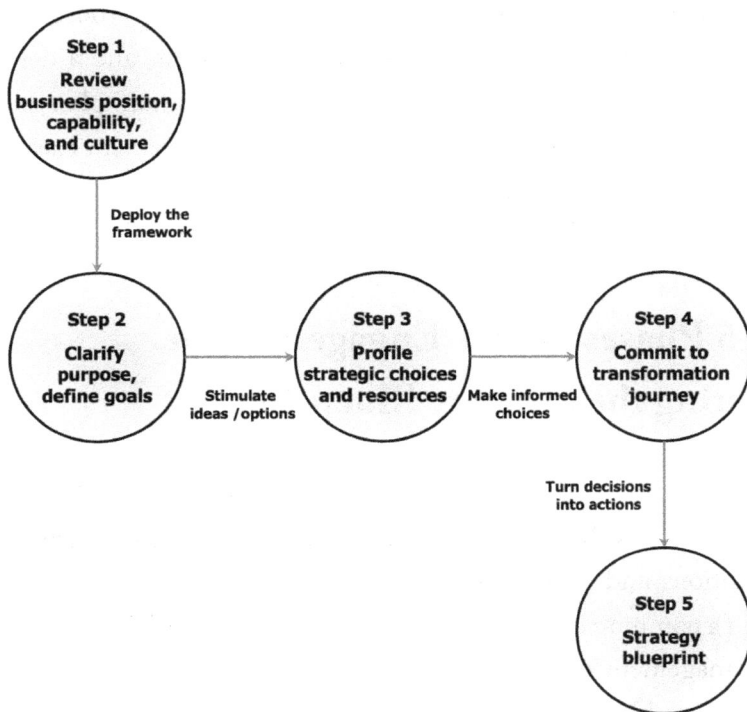

Phase 1: Establish the Baseline

To prepare for a robust strategic review, a comprehensive set of insights is gathered that serves as the foundation for informed decision-making. It begins with analysing historical financial performance to understand revenue trends, cost structures, profitability and cash flow. The financial data provides context for past successes as well as current constraints.

In parallel, customer research, including surveys, interviews, and behavioural analysis provides insights into customer needs, satisfaction and loyalty drivers. This should be paired with a competitor analysis, benchmarking direct and indirect competitors across offerings, pricing and market share to inform overall positioning. A clear picture of the business's market positioning helps identify how to build differentiation and address perception gaps. At the same time, an assessment of industry trends, from technology shifts to evolving customer expectations, prepares the organisation for future disruptions and opportunities. A PESTLE analysis (Political, Economic, Social, Technological, Legal, Environmental) provides a structured lens to profile external macro factors, which are scored to reflect their impact on strategic choices later in the process.[2]

Internally, a review of capabilities (people, processes, systems and culture) evaluates the organisation's readiness to execute strategy. This includes assessing the quality of leadership, innovation, delivery efficiency and scalability. Identifying key success factors and those conditions necessary to thrive rather than merely survive within your chosen industry helps narrow the focus on what really matters to secure a competitive advantage.

Bringing these elements together, the SLT conducts a SWOT analysis (Strengths, Weaknesses, Opportunities, Threats) to summarise internal and external insights. The SWOT provides a strategic snapshot, helping the SLT assess where the company stands today and offering the first clues as to where the business should consider focusing collective efforts in the future.

Assembling these ingredients creates a balanced, fact-based platform in the form of a "data book" for the SLT to base strategy conversations around. Its purpose is to arrive at a shared understanding of where there is alignment on common factors and where differences of interpretation exist. This step is critical to stimulating constructive conflict and strategic thinking on the current realities and future direction of travel. Completing a thorough preparation process ensures that goal setting and strategy formulation are rooted in real-world insights – built on data rather than assumptions, intuition or bias.

Phase 2: Setting Strategic Goals and Outlining Options

The second phase involves defining the future destination for the business and exploring multiple pathways to get there. The work of this phase is distinguished by:

The expression of vision and mission. While the business will likely already have a vision and mission, this phase often involves revisiting and refining what is expressed to ensure that what has been crafted is still relevant and inspiring.

Defining strategic goals. The SLT sets three-year strategic goals that reflect the business's ambitions. These should be measurable, time-bound and sufficiently bold to stretch the organisation. Strategic objectives should not be confused with BHAGs (Big, Hairy, Audacious Goals), which have a much longer 20-25 year time frame. However, BHAGs may help inspire the essence of what becomes the 3-year strategic goals.

Generating strategic options. With strategic goals in place, the SLT starts to consider different strategic pathways and address questions on how to achieve growth: Should the company focus on geographic expansion, or product innovation focussed around selling more to existing customers, or acquisition of a competitor or channel partner, or expansion into new markets with a unique offer that leverages internal core competencies which provide a distinct advantage?

Assessing trade-offs. Each strategic option carries implications for investment, risk and capability requirements. The SLT weighs these trade-offs to ensure strategies are prioritised, feasible and aligned with organisational strengths, and in doing so, forms a view on the acceptance criteria on which to base alternative strategic choices.

This phase culminates in a strategic outline that defines where the SLT agrees the business should be in three years and outlines the specifics of how long it will take to achieve this goal.

An excellent framework to employ during this phase of work is the "strategic choice cascade" set out in *Playing to Win* by Roger Martin[3] described on the next page:

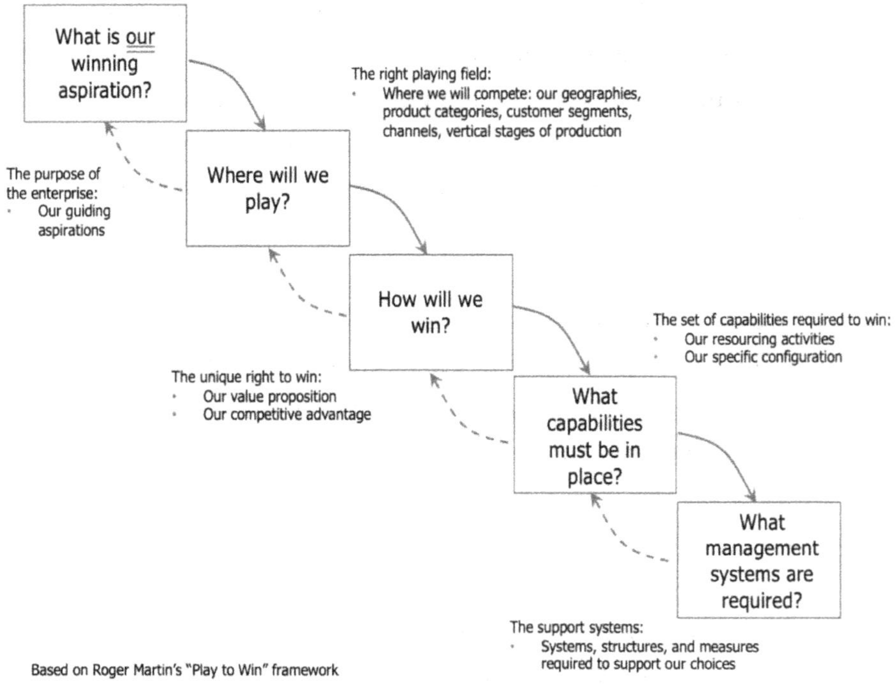
What is our winning aspiration?
The purpose of the enterprise:
• Our guiding aspirations
Where will we play?
The right playing field:
• Where we will compete: our geographies, product categories, customer segments, channels, vertical stages of production
How will we win?
The unique right to win:
• Our value proposition
• Our competitive advantage
What capabilities must be in place?
The set of capabilities required to win:
• Our resourcing activities
• Our specific configuration
What management systems are required?
The support systems:
• Systems, structures, and measures required to support our choices
Based on Roger Martin's "Play to Win" framework

To achieve a mature conclusion, it is often advantageous to engage an external facilitator to apply a strategy development framework, such as "Playing to Win," and help guide the thinking process. One of the primary benefits of doing so is the ability to maintain objectivity. SLT leaders often bring valuable experience, but also assumptions, biases or attachments to legacy thinking. A neutral facilitator can challenge the status quo without the weight of internal politics or history and encourage more open, honest and fundamental conversations by surfacing tensions or blind spots that might otherwise go unspoken.

Critically, a skilled facilitator can also ensure that all voices are heard and help align the SLT around a shared vision, rather than one dominated by the loudest or most senior voice in the room. By the end of the process, the SLT not only has a refined vision but also a clear sense of ownership and commitment to it. A facilitator can also help structure a communication plan once the strategic plan is developed and keep the SLT honest about rollout to the business by holding the team to account. Sadly, this critical step is often overlooked.

An external facilitator may also bring a broader perspective, introducing creative problem-solving techniques and insights gained from working with similar businesses in different industries. They can offer fresh ideas, benchmarks and innovative thinking that internal teams may not be exposed to. This is particularly useful when exploring alternative routes forward and introducing options that stretch thinking beyond the "safe" and familiar. Ultimately, the role of an external facilitator is to help the SLT lift their heads from day-to-day operations, zoom out and co-create a vision that is ambitious, cohesive and achievable – along with the pathways most likely to realise it.

Phase 3: Building Consensus Around the Value Proposition

With goals and strategic options defined, the SLT enters a third phase, which is centred on alignment. This is where the SLT moves from exploring possibilities to making commitments.

Refining the value proposition. The SLT reached consensus on the business's value proposition and how it is expressed through products and services. This is not merely a marketing statement, but a deeply understood expression of how the company creates value for customers that is distinctive. An external facilitator's neutrality adds value at this juncture, as they can moderate passions, emotions and biases within an SLT.

Organisation role clarity. With the value proposition as a guiding anchor, the SLT maps how each organisation unit contributes to its delivery. The SLT should not shy away from asking itself direct questions, such as what does marketing need to do differently? How must operations evolve? This challenging questioning process helps avoid resource overlaps and ensures all departments are aligned.

Cross-functional integration. During this phase of work, the SLT is building collaboration between departments, identifying interdependencies and highlighting accountabilities. These conversations are crucial for cohesive execution.

Shared ownership. By involving each SLT leader in shaping the strategy blueprint, the SLT builds shared ownership. This increases the likelihood that strategies will be championed and cascaded effectively throughout the organisation, and avoids the helpless shrug, which indicates what is being asked is "nothing to do with me."

This phase ensures that the strategy is not just visionary but also operationally coherent. The conversations are frequently demanding. It can feel like an uncomfortable and bruising process, as these discussions often force SLT leaders to confront inconvenient truths about performance gaps, misaligned priorities or the limitations of current structures and capabilities.

To participate effectively, SLT leaders must move beyond organisational silos and personal agendas, and assume collective accountability to openly debate how roles, responsibilities and resources may change going forward. The level of detail encourages a shared commitment, which may reveal differing interpretations of the company's direction or resistance to change. Tensions often arise when previously unspoken issues tied to uneven accountability, overlapping authority or historical friction between departments come to the surface.

SLT leaders are naturally defensive when their teams' capabilities or ways of working are scrutinised and found wanting – but they need to "let it go." This is what collaboration within a functioning SLT really looks and feels like.

The process can be emotionally taxing and should not be rushed. It always takes longer than expected because it requires SLT leaders to relinquish what they think they each control and co-create a shared future, rather than protecting turf or legacy positions. Difficult conversations build trust, expose hidden risks, and, when managed constructively, result in strategies that are not only ambitious but also executable when supported by the entire leadership team.

Committing a business to a chosen direction requires more than strategic clarity – it demands the engagement of both hearts and minds. While logic and data help build the case for change, emotional buy-in is what drives commitment, resilience and sustained effort.

People need to believe in the "why," feel connected to purpose and see their role in the journey. When hearts become engaged, teams move from compliance to ownership. An SLT that embraces this principle ensures the strategy is fully understood and is motivated to bring it to life every day.

The adage "train hard, fight easy" is relevant here. If the SLT is not actively working to surface and resolve issues during the planning phases, they are likely to continue avoiding conflict and diverge when it comes to execution. If planning is "too easy," it is a warning that execution may not align.

Phase 4: Committing to The Journey

The fourth phase focuses on execution planning. Having defined the strategy and aligned the organisation, the SLT must now ensure that there are shared structures and standard processes in place to implement effectively:

> **Annual goals.** The three-year goals are broken down into annual goals. These can then be translated into quarterly OKRs at the corporate, functional and individual levels. OKRs create alignment, focus and accountability and stimulate action and can form a highly effective backbone of a management execution system.[4]

> **Strategic scorecard.** The SLT agrees on a scorecard that tracks progress against key leading and lagging performance indicators (KPIs) tied to strategic goals. According to data availability, the scorecard enables real-time performance monitoring and course

correction for use in weekly, monthly and quarterly review meetings.

Operating rhythm. Regular check-ins, weekly trackers, quarterly reviews and strategy refresh sessions are established as part of the organisation's rhythm. This keeps the strategy top-of-mind as well as responsive to change.

Storytelling. The SLT develops a compelling story to communicate the strategy to the broader business.[5] This narrative connects the dots between vision, strategy, department and individual contributions. It is structured in such a way that employees not only come to understand the firm's strategy but also become engaged with it and are inspired to act on it. Storytelling merits investment in creative treatments that bring what may be perceived as "solid but dry" material alive so that a wider internal audience can appreciate their role in execution. Bringing in external communications expertise to help bring the story to life in a way that resonates deeply with employees is often a step that transforms an honest endeavour into an uplifting call to action.

Leadership commitment. Perhaps most critically, this phase solidifies the SLT's commitment to the strategy. The SLT emphasise priorities in their respective communications with their teams and holds them accountable for delivery by showing frequent participation with high engagement in execution and its review.

When an SLT commits to a firm's strategy, the impact is profound, and the SLT can naturally "walk the talk" with authority, modelling the desired behaviours for others to adopt. By setting clear, actionable targets for the year, the business gains a unified direction – ensuring that everyone is working toward the same goals. Tracking progress regularly provides a way to measure success and make data-driven decisions, and presenting the strategy as a compelling and relatable story makes it more appealing.

When team members understand the company's mission and how their individual roles contribute to the larger vision, they feel more connected. A well-told story transforms strategy into something actionable and meaningful, helping the SLT drive execution by bringing the strategy to life.

Phase 5: Documenting the Strategy Blueprint

Organisations that invest the time and energy in developing a comprehensive strategy blueprint in written form – and not in glitzy charts, fluffy concepts or clever and inspiring sayings – reap significant benefits.[6] The written word signals attention to detail and provides an audit trail that everyone can check. The strategy blueprint facilitates:

Unified direction. Everyone is aligned around a common direction, which reduces friction and increases efficiency.

Increased agility. With clear priorities and the adoption of a coherent management execution system, the organisation can respond quickly to change without losing sight of its strategic goals.

Stronger culture. A shared vision and values reinforce a strong, purpose-driven culture.

Improved performance. By linking strategy to execution through KPIs and OKRs, organisations drive higher performance and better outcomes.

Enhanced accountability. With clear goals and transparent tracking, accountability becomes embedded in the organisation's DNA.

In an age of uncertainty and rapid change, the ability to define and execute a clear strategy is a key differentiator. A strategy blueprint is the asset that provides the structure and clarity needed to navigate complexity, inspire teams and deliver sustained performance.

The role of the SLT is central to this process. By working together over the five described phases – establishing a baseline informed by data, goal setting and option generation, achieving consensus on how value is secured, committing to the journey and documenting the outcome in the form of a coherent strategy blueprint that links all the components – the SLT ensures that strategy is not just a document but a living expression of reality.

The strategy blueprint becomes more than a planning tool. It becomes a shared language for decision-making, a compass for prioritisation and a catalyst for performance. The strategy blueprint becomes the SLT's playbook. Once complete, the SLT can lead with purpose, coherence and conviction – and bring the entire organisation along on the journey.

An Illustration of a Strategy Blueprint: "Studio Nova," A Creative Agency

Company Overview

Studio Nova is a mid-sized creative agency specialising in branding, digital content and experiential marketing for lifestyle, fashion and tech brands. After rapid early growth, the agency is now facing increasing competition, shifting client demands and the need to mature its internal operations.

Setting Strategic Goals and Outlining Options

Vision

To be the most sought-after creative partner for culture-driven brands, shaping the future.

Mission

We amplify brands by crafting bold, immersive experiences that connect with real people in real moments.

Three-Year Strategic Goals

1. Double revenue through both client acquisition and increased account value.

2. Expand capabilities to include content production and influencer management.

3. Achieve operational excellence with scalable systems and predictable delivery models.

Strategic Options Explored

- Geographic expansion: Open a Northern office to tap into the tech/lifestyle ecosystem.

- New service launch: Build an in-house content studio for video and motion graphics.

- Partnership model: Partner with influencer agencies to co-deliver campaigns.

- System integration: Develop a proprietary project tracking and client portal.

The SLT chooses a hybrid path: to expand services and improve operations before undertaking geographic expansion.

Alignment on Refined Value Proposition and Functional Roles

Studio Nova is a cultural creative partner that fuses strategy, storytelling and real-world experience to create brand impact that resonates.

This statement clarified their shift from being just a creative supplier to a brand partner, which reframed how sales, account management and creative should interact.

Functional Alignment

- The strategy team shifted from being reactive brief-takers to embedded client advisors.

- The creative department developed modular creative models to work faster with client feedback.

- Operations introduced project lifecycle mapping to standardise timelines.

- Business development now leads with value proposition-based storytelling, not just portfolios that describe capabilities.

Cross-functional initiatives include:

- Forming "Creative Pods" (strategy + design + production)
- Unified briefing and feedback tools across departments
- Shared KPIs for team delivery, not just individual performance

Implementation Plan with Scorecard, OKRs and Supporting Narrative

Strategic Scorecard

Strategic Goal	KPI	Target
Revenue growth	Year-on-year revenue increase	+20% annually
Capability expansion	% of revenue from new services not yet in market	30% by Year 3
Operational excellence	Project delivery predictability: time and cost	95%
Employee engagement	eNPS (employee net promoter score)	>50

Annual Goals

- Introduce key account management processes designed to grow revenue by 20% from existing clients.

- Partner with a lead generation firm to secure new business and start working with six more ideal clients by year's end.

- Launch new content production services focused on video and more dynamic content generation approaches to add 20% to revenue by year's end.

- Improve project delivery predictability so that 95% of projects are delivered on time and within budget.

Story for Communication

A compelling internal narrative is crafted:

"From Studio to Partner: How Nova Is evolving to be the creative ally of tomorrow's leading brands."

This message was conveyed through "town halls" (all-staff company events), onboarding and team meetings, emphasising the shift from being a reactive service agency to a proactive strategic partner. The story was personalised with client wins and testimonials that reflect the benefits of different ways of working to build belief.

Operating Rhythm

- Quarterly strategy reviews with progress on OKRs

- Monthly team retrospectives to refine ways of working

- Annual strategy refresh tied to client trend analysis

Final Result: A Cohesive, Actionable Blueprint

Studio Nova's SLT emerged with:

- A shared direction rooted in purpose and competitive edge

- A coordinated cross-functional operating model

- Annual goals and OKRs that engage employees to turn vision into action

- A communication engine that engages hearts and minds

5 Reasons A Strategy Blueprint Makes a Real Difference

1. **Clarity of purpose.** A strategy blueprint formalises the company's purpose and long-term aspirations. By documenting a shared vision, mission and values, the strategy blueprint provides clarity on why the business exists, what it stands for and where it is headed.

2. **Alignment across and within organisational units.** A strategy blueprint ensures that all functions, departments, teams and individuals understand their role in delivering the strategy. This alignment is crucial for preventing siloed thinking and promoting collaboration.

3. **Strategic focus.** The strategy blueprint enables the SLT to focus on a few key strategic goals, rather than being distracted by competing priorities. It allows resource allocation and effort to be directed where they will make the greatest impact.

4. **Operational guidance.** By including an operating structure and implementation plan, the strategy blueprint provides a roadmap for translating strategy into action.

5. **Performance measurement.** Through annual goals and OKRs, the strategy blueprint establishes a mechanism for tracking progress, adjusting course and holding individuals and teams accountable.

Summary

For any strategy to succeed, it must be both coherent and cohesive, and anchored in clear thinking and shared ownership. A strategy blueprint co-created by the SLT provides clarity of direction, coupled with a genuine commitment to execution. When leaders shape the strategy together, they align around shared priorities, challenge assumptions early and build the resolve required to deliver results.

Effective strategy development and planning typically unfold in five key phases:

1. **Setting the baseline** and understanding current performance, market dynamics and organisational capability

2. **Setting goals and exploring options**; defining ambition and evaluating strategic choices

3. **Engineering the value proposition** and sharpening how the organisation creates distinctive value for customers and how success is measured

4. **Detailing the implementation plan** by mapping out initiatives, resources and benefits

5. **Turning the strategy into a story** and crafting a compelling narrative that inspires both employees and customers

When strategy is built in this way, it becomes more than a document – it becomes a shared commitment to a bolder and better future.

Reflective Questions

The questions set out below are designed to help you internalise key ideas, examine your own experiences in light of what you've read and consider how any insights might shape your thinking and actions in future. There are no right answers – only honest ones. Use these opportunities to reflect, deepen your awareness, spark conversation with others or simply increase awareness of what's changing for you as you make progress through this book.

> Do all the parts of our strategy – vision, mission, values, goals and key initiatives – tell a consistent story?

> Is the strategy bold enough to inspire but focused enough to execute?

> Have we ensured joint ownership of cross-functional initiatives, rather than leaving them in "no man's land"?

> Does everyone – from SLT to "front line" – understand how their work contributes to the strategy?

> Do we have the operating model and infrastructure to deliver what we're aiming for?

There is a longer list of questions in the "Appendix: Reflective Questions." These are designed to be addressed when you, with or without the team, have more time available for reflection, rather than reaction.

Chapter 7
Crossing the Knowing-Doing Gap

"I don't think eliminating the knowing–doing gap depends on the amount of knowledge around, but depends much more on people's attitudes and intentions. Do they actually want to turn knowledge into action or just go through the motions of acting as if they are busy or are accomplishing something?"
– Jeffrey Pfeffer, Academic

Every business leader knows the frustration of seeing smart strategies and good ideas fail to translate into meaningful action. The gap between knowing what to do and actually doing it is what Jeffrey Pfeffer and Robert Sutton call the "knowing–doing gap."[1] It is one of the most persistent challenges in modern organisations. Too often, this gap is not due to a lack of intelligence or insight, but to a fear of change, unclear priorities, weak accountability or a culture that rewards talk over traction.

This chapter examines how senior leadership teams can bridge that gap by fostering a high-trust, high-discipline execution culture. At the heart of this is the adoption of a management execution system that connects strategy to action in real time. A core function of the senior leadership team (SLT) is to design and implement a management process that connects daily activities with strategic goals – ensuring that what people do each day is tied directly to the outcomes the organisation seeks. When teams are clear about what matters most, empowered to own results and supported with the right rhythms and reporting, the organisation moves faster and with more focus. Execution becomes part of the culture – not a scramble at year-end to "make the numbers."

More than just a framework, Objectives and Key Results (OKRs) can become a transformative way of working when well deployed. They reinforce intentional leadership, effective delegation, clear accountability and a performance culture rooted in shared values. This chapter demonstrates how to integrate that thinking into day–to–day operations, transforming strategy from a slide deck into shared outcomes, and aligning rewards, recognition and leadership behaviours around what truly matters.

The knowing–doing gap is not an inevitable modern-day phenomenon. The tools to close it are within reach, but need to be applied consistently. By embedding execution discipline into "how we work," an effective management execution system eliminates the drift between good ideas and actual performance. In short, it turns "we should be doing" into "we are doing" – and that's the conversation that gets things done.

OKRs: A Good Place to Start

The OKRs framework, popularised by leading companies such as Google, Intel and LinkedIn, offers a powerful approach to transforming how businesses execute strategy – by improving focus, driving action, enhancing accountability and enabling transparent communication. OKRs also help address the more nuanced challenge of delegation by highlighting the balance between employee competency and managerial control.

OKRs are a goal-setting framework that helps businesses define clear objectives and measure progress through specific, quantifiable key results. An objective outlines a significant, qualitative goal to be achieved, while key results provide measurable outcomes that indicate achievement. The simplicity and rigour of OKRs drive strategic clarity and operational focus.

For SLTs, adopting OKRs as a management execution system is not merely a procedural shift – it can represent a cultural transformation. By linking day-to-day operations with overarching strategic priorities, OKRs act as a bridge between goals and execution. They ensure that every team member understands not only what needs to be done but why it matters.

One of the most significant benefits of OKRs is their ability to sharpen organisational focus. In many companies, competing priorities and a lack of alignment often dilute effort. OKRs counter this by forcing teams and individuals to identify and commit to a few high-impact objectives each cycle – typically no more than three to five.

This disciplined focus encourages SLTs to engage in more thoughtful prioritisation and avoid the trap of trying to do everything at once. In my experience, SLTs become more deliberate in choosing where to invest time, energy and resources when using OKRs. The increased clarity reduces noise and distraction, making it easier for teams and individuals to channel their efforts toward activities that truly "move the needle."

Moreover, with regular reporting, the visibility of OKRs across a business builds alignment. When everyone can see what others are working on, overlaps are minimised and the synergies across work are amplified. This collective visibility ensures that energy is not only focused but leveraged and harmonised.

OKRs work by empowering employees and giving them ownership of outcomes rather than prescribing detailed tasks. This autonomy encourages individuals to be proactive, innovative and reach out to collaborate and problem-solve, building a culture where action is valued. When employees set their own key results (within the boundaries of team or company objectives), they are more likely to feel a sense of accountability and motivation. OKRs create an environment where individuals are encouraged to think critically about how they can contribute to the organisation's success – within the guard rails of the overall strategy.

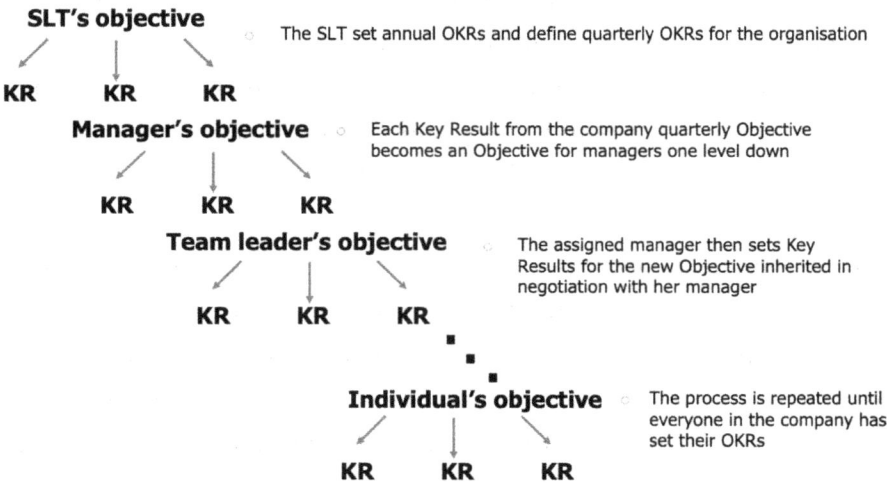

SLT's objective The SLT set annual OKRs and define quarterly OKRs for the organisation

KR   KR   KR

Manager's objective Each Key Result from the company quarterly Objective becomes an Objective for managers one level down

KR   KR   KR

Team leader's objective The assigned manager then sets Key Results for the new Objective inherited in negotiation with her manager

KR   KR   KR

Individual's objective The process is repeated until everyone in the company has set their OKRs

KR   KR   KR

For SLTs, this shift means moving from directive to intentional leadership (see Chapter 4). Rather than micromanaging, SLT leaders define the destination and empower teams to chart the path. This approach not only accelerates execution but also builds internal capacity for problem-solving, decision-making and leadership at all levels of the organisation.

Accountability in many organisations is often fuzzy. Performance reviews are retrospective, and ownership of results can be ambiguous. OKRs bring accountability to the forefront and keep it current by making goals explicit, time-bound and measurable.

Each key result becomes a commitment – a promise to achieve a specific outcome within a defined timeframe. As OKRs and the steps towards their achievement are regularly reviewed (weekly, monthly, quarterly), they create a rhythm of accountability that is both ongoing and forward-looking. For an SLT, this dynamic provides a real-time dashboard of progress, allowing the team to spot issues early and intervene proactively. It also establishes a shared language of performance, where success is not judged solely by effort or intent, but by measurable impact.

This clarity changes the nature of accountability conversations. Rather than subjective appraisals, discussions are grounded in objective data and evidence. This not only depersonalises feedback but "keeps it real" by enhancing fairness and objectivity.

Effective execution relies on clear and consistent communication. Despite all the "best practices" and multiple available communication applications, many organisations still suffer from communication silos and misaligned messaging. OKRs provide a common framework for discussing goals, progress and challenges. As OKRs are visible to the entire business, they democratise information. Employees understand how their work connects to broader goals, and leaders gain insight into real-time team-level progress and obstacles.

This mutual visibility makes for crisper conversations and injects pace. OKRs help individuals articulate their work more clearly and effectively. When everyone speaks the same language of objectives and key results, conversations become more focused, productive and impactful.

Regular check-ins are not just about reporting progress – the supporting reporting systems do that. They are opportunities to discuss challenges, request support and share learnings, whilst flagging risks and delays. Based on fact-based conversations using verifiable data, SLT leaders can identify and address bottlenecks, allocating resources where they are most needed.

Beyond immediate execution benefits, OKRs help instil transparency and promote continuous improvement. Because OKRs emphasise outcomes – not just activities – they expose what is working and what is not. Missed key results are not viewed as failures, but rather as learning opportunities. Quarterly retrospectives allow teams to identify barriers to success, reflect on what slowed progress and brainstorm what can be learned and done differently. This iterative learning mindset enhances organisational agility and resilience, while also building core skills within individuals.

SLT leaders play a critical role in leading the way in these conversations. When leaders are open about their own OKRs, share progress candidly and acknowledge challenges, they create a safe environment for others to do the same. This vulnerability drives authenticity and psychological safety – key ingredients for engagement and innovation (see Chapter 2).

OKRs are a management execution system and represent a powerful approach to securing traction in a business. OKRs do not replace strategy; they help deliver it.[2]

Imagine for a moment that you work for a shipping company that employs multiple drivers and delivery people. As the use of autonomous vehicles grows across the industry's value chain, you need to respond to this radical change or be left behind. Your goal could include increasing the number of packages each person delivers. Your goal could be to reduce the time it takes to deliver each package. Your goal might also involve increasing automation in your delivery services.

Question: Which goal should the business teams work on? Each of these can make an excellent OKR – but only the ones that align with the strategy actually matter.

If the strategy is to "get with the times" and automate, you will set goals that reflect that direction. If you plan to optimise the utilisation of your existing workforce, you'll set different goals. OKRs are not a strategy. Without a strategy, you could adopt excellent OKRs that become a triumph of activity over productivity – and risk damaging the business.

Delegation Dilemma:
Balancing Competency and Control

Effective delegation is a fundamental building block of leadership excellence, yet it remains a nuanced challenge. Managers often struggle with the tension between empowering employees and ensuring outcomes. A research study (CIPD, 2017)[3] highlights that around half of HR professionals believe senior leaders lack the people management behaviours and skills to get the best from their people. Leaders are often more focused on subject matter expertise than leadership expertise. This tension becomes particularly acute in high-stakes environments, where failure has significant consequences.

OKRs help provide a structured approach to delegation. When tasks are delegated with clear objectives and measurable results, ambiguity is minimised. However, the success of this delegation still depends on two key variables: the employee's competency and the level of control the manager retains. If an employee has high competency, less control may be necessary – the manager can focus on defining the outcome and trust the individual to determine the how. On the other hand, when competency is lower or the task is complex, the manager may need to exercise greater oversight. In both cases, the objective remains the same: the employee owns the work objective and how it is completed.

This dynamic can be visualised through the delegation continuum[4] (see below), which depicts the spectrum ranging from "direct control" to "empowered autonomy." OKRs help anchor this continuum by clarifying what must be achieved, allowing managers to adjust their approach to achieve the desired outcome based on an employee's capabilities.

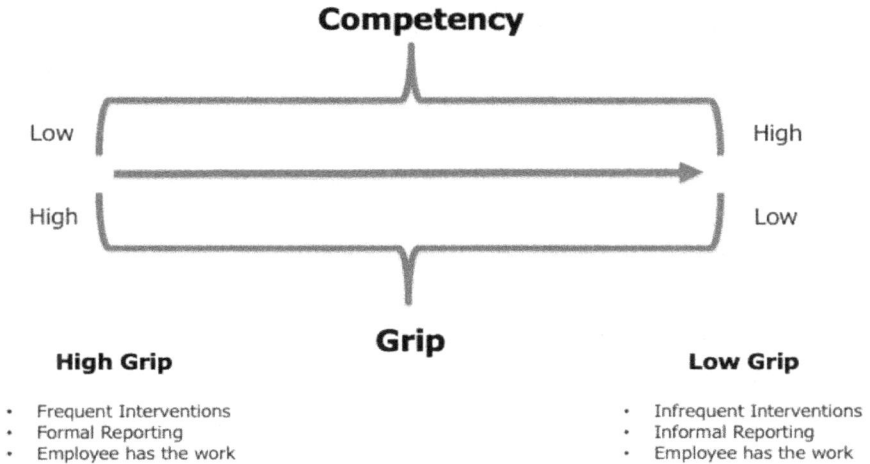

Competency

High Grip		Low Grip
Low		High
High		Low

Grip

High Grip
- Frequent Interventions
- Formal Reporting
- Employee has the work

Low Grip
- Infrequent Interventions
- Informal Reporting
- Employee has the work

OKRs create the checkpoints that allow for course correction without undermining autonomy. Instead of waiting for a project or work activity to be completed to evaluate success, regular OKR reviews enable managers to intervene early, provide support and recalibrate expectations as needed. This balance of trust and verification is key to scaling execution. SLTs that master this dynamic create organisations where accountability is clearly defined and leadership is distributed.

Adopting OKRs as the chosen management execution system is not a case of "cut and paste" – it requires careful design and disciplined execution. The following tips can help an SLT achieve successful adoption:

Start with strategic alignment. Ensure organisational OKRs are based on the stated mission and shared strategic goals, summarised as the business's annual goals.

Cascade with flexibility. Allow teams to align their OKRs with top-level goals, while exercising intentional leadership and encouraging autonomy in defining how to achieve them.

Limit the number. Focus on a few (ideally no more than three) impactful OKRs to avoid overextension.

Create a cadence to embed OKRs in conversations. Establish regular check-ins to review progress, address blockers and celebrate wins. Touchpoints can include weekly "on/off track" updates, monthly reviews and more in-depth one-to-one conversations.

Use tools and transparency. Leverage digital tools to track OKRs and make them visible to all. If your business has over 150 FTEs, definitely trade up from using spreadsheets to a reporting platform closely aligned with your adopted approach to OKRs.

Model from the top. SLTs must visibly commit to their own OKRs and demonstrate accountability – people will be looking for it. The SLT's commitment is fundamental to success and the key influence on the quality of performance culture experienced by all.

For SLTs, adopting OKRs as the central management execution system is both a strategic imperative and a leadership opportunity. By embedding OKRs into the fabric of the business, SLTs can transform not only how goals are set and measured, but also how people work, collaborate and grow. They offer a powerful mechanism for aligning vision with action – and, managed well, ensure that everyone is moving in the same direction with clarity, purpose and energy.

Deloitte reports (2024) that companies using OKRs improved their ability to pivot and respond to change compared to those with traditional planning cycles.[5] There are numerous examples of businesses reporting benefits such as improved clarity, customer satisfaction, execution, employee retention, cross-functional alignment and faster growth. Deloitte notes a 2.5x greater revenue growth in companies with well-aligned OKRs.[6]

Early adopters of OKRs – such as Google – openly share their successes and learnings from adopting the OKR framework on YouTube[7] and elsewhere. Google is possibly the most cited example of success with OKRs. According to John Doerr, who introduced OKRs to Google, the approach allowed the company to maintain alignment across rapidly growing teams, stay focused while scaling fast and encourage ambitious goal setting ("moonshots") while measuring progress with clarity. The results speak for themselves: Google scaled from 40 FTEs to over 100,000 employees without losing alignment and agility.

Reward & Recognition

Creating and sustaining a high-performance culture requires more than strategy and a robust management execution system. It requires the deliberate reinforcement of the behaviours that drive excellence.

SLTs play a pivotal role in shaping culture through reward and recognition systems that align organisational values with strategic goals. When done well, these systems reinforce desired behaviours, motivate teams and elevate engagement.

The first step in institutionalising a reward and recognition system is ensuring it reflects and supports the desired culture. Traditional rewards, such as tenure-based bonuses or generic employee-of-the-month programs, often fall short because they reward presence rather than performance. To build a performance-oriented operating culture, SLTs need to directly link recognition to specific achievements, outcomes and behaviours that exemplify the desired results.

This linkage creates a virtuous cycle: when employees see that high performance and values-driven behaviour are recognised and rewarded, they are more likely to replicate and sustain them. The culture, in turn, becomes self-reinforcing.

Effective reward systems combine both intrinsic and extrinsic motivators. Extrinsic rewards – such as bonuses, promotions and non-monetary gifts – are tangible acknowledgements of achievement. Intrinsic rewards – such as personal growth, meaningful work and public recognition – are equally powerful, particularly in knowledge-driven or creative environments. SLTs must ensure that their system is not skewed toward transactional incentives alone. A narrow focus on monetary rewards can crowd out intrinsic motivation, leading to short-termism and unhealthy competition. Instead, a balanced approach rewards both outcomes and the values-driven behaviours that lead to sustainable performance.

Examples of intrinsic rewards include:

- Public praise during team meetings or town halls

- Peer-to-peer recognition platforms, e.g. "cheers for peers"

- Opportunities for skill development or mentorship

- Assignments to high-profile and high-impact projects, especially around innovation

Extrinsic rewards might include:

- Performance-based bonuses

- Gift cards or additional paid time off

- Secondments and other career advancement opportunities

- Invitations to leadership development programmes

While results matter, the path taken to achieve them is just as important in a performance culture. Recognising only outcomes can inadvertently encourage corner-cutting, siloed behaviour or unhealthy competition. SLTs must reinforce not only *what* was achieved, but also *how* it was achieved.

This means celebrating behaviours such as:

- Collaboration and team support

- Proactive problem-solving

- Customer-centred thinking

- Continuous improvement

- Adaptability and resilience under pressure

Recognition programmes should be structured to include both formal and informal channels. A formal programme might consist of a quarterly "values in action" award, where employees nominate peers who have exemplified the organisation's core behaviours. Informal recognition – such as a personalised thank-you note from an SLT leader or a shout-out in a team chat – should be equally encouraged, as it builds day-to-day cultural momentum.

A reward system that is perceived as opaque or biased can damage morale and erode trust. For SLTs, ensuring fairness and transparency is critical to the credibility and effectiveness of recognition efforts.

Key principles include:

Explicit criteria for recognition. Define what constitutes exemplary behaviour or performance.

Consistent application. Ensure managers across functions and beyond the Head Office apply the same standards.

Broad accessibility. Include opportunities for recognition across all roles and levels.

Inclusive design. Avoid systems that only reward highly visible roles; include support staff, project-based contributors and frontline workers.

Involving employees in the design and review of the system can also enhance trust and buy-in. When people feel heard, they are more likely to engage with and believe in the system.

To help reinforce strategic alignment, SLTs must ensure that rewards and recognition support not only individual performance but also team and company-wide objectives. This requires embedding recognition criteria within the strategic planning and performance management frameworks. So, if innovation is a key strategic goal, recognition systems should highlight and reward experimentation, idea generation and calculated risk-taking. If customer experience is a top priority, then behaviours that improve service quality or delight customers should be spotlighted.

Supervisors and first-level managers are often the frontline agents of recognition – yet many struggle with how, when and whom to recognise. To become effective recognition champions, these managers usually require training and tools. Otherwise, expectations heaped upon them by SLTs can sound like hollow rhetoric.

This includes:

- Educating managers on the value and impact of recognition

- Providing materials or prompts for timely and meaningful feedback

- Encouraging managers to individualise recognition based on employee preferences

Managers should also be encouraged to celebrate progress, not just results. Recognising milestones along the way helps maintain high motivation and fosters a growth mindset.

Peer recognition can be a powerful complement to top-down rewards. Colleagues often witness everyday acts of leadership, collaboration and effort that managers may not see. Empowering employees to recognise one another helps democratise appreciation and foster a deeper sense of community.

SLTs can help institutionalise this by:

- Implementing digital platforms that allow employees to share praise

- Creating informal "kudos" systems within teams or departments

- Including peer nominations in formal recognition awards

Such initiatives foster mutual respect and elevate the visibility of behind-the-scenes contributions.

To ensure that the reward and recognition system remains effective, SLTs must regularly and intelligently measure its impact and iterate accordingly. However, beware of "over-goaling" this activity – it may lead to misuse of the system.

Metrics to bear in mind may include:

- Employee engagement and satisfaction scores

- Participation rates in recognition programmes

- Performance data correlated with recognition activity

- Feedback from employee pulse surveys

In the early stages of my career, when late nights and weekend working were required to hit deadlines, being offered the chance to take my wife out for dinner at the company's expense was more than just a perk – it was a meaningful gesture of appreciation. After long hours, tight deadlines and constant travel, these opportunities felt like a valued breath of fresh air. Sharing a fine meal in an elegant venue, free from the usual financial calculations, was a moment of gratitude. It served as a reminder that the company recognised not just professional dedication, but the personal sacrifices made along the way. For my wife, it was a glimpse into the appreciation I received – and showed that the company cared. Showing care in this way made it easier to accept moments when extra effort was called upon in the future. Whilst support at home may not always have been forthcoming, at least the understanding was there.

A performance culture does not emerge by accident – it is intentionally built and actively maintained. For SLTs, institutionalising a thoughtful, equitable and strategically aligned reward and recognition system is a critical lever in this endeavour. By reinforcing both results and the behaviours that drive them, recognition systems not only motivate employees but also embed the organisation's values into everyday work.

In doing so, SLTs cultivate an environment where people feel seen, valued and empowered to perform at their best. This culture of appreciation becomes a strategic asset – one that fuels engagement, drives results and builds lasting organisational resilience.

Summary

Many organisations struggle with the knowing–doing gap – the disconnect between strategic intent and actual execution. SLT leaders often know most of what needs to be done but lack the structure, focus or follow-through to address gaps as they appear and respond with the necessary actions to make it happen. This is where OKRs can provide real value. By translating strategic goals into clear, measurable outcomes, OKRs offer a disciplined framework for review, action and accountability.

A core strength of OKRs is that they tap into the principles of intentional leadership (see Chapter 4), encouraging leaders to practise effective delegation that empowers teams and individuals to take ownership of outcomes while staying aligned to overarching goals. OKRs also promote regular communication, enabling leaders and teams to track progress, adjust priorities and course-correct in real-time. Feedback and recognition tied to measurable progress help maintain high momentum and ensure achievements are visible and celebrated.

Used well, OKRs bridge the gap between knowing and doing – and turn good intentions into consistent execution.

Reflective Questions

The questions set out below are designed to help you internalise key ideas, examine your own experiences in light of what you've read and consider how any insights might shape your thinking and actions in future. There are no correct answers – only honest ones. Use these opportunities to reflect, deepen your awareness, spark conversation with others or simply increase awareness of what's changing for you as you make progress through this book.

> How do we ensure visibility and transparency of goals, progress and outcomes at every level of the organisation?

> How do we ensure that delegation does not become abdication – or micromanagement?

> Do we recognise both the achievement of results and the demonstration of values-driven behaviours in performance conversations?

> Is recognition timely, specific and meaningful to the recipient?

> Are we, as leaders, seen as approachable, supportive and consistent in reinforcing performance culture principles?

There is a longer list of questions in the "Appendix: Reflective Questions." These are designed to be addressed when you, with or without the team, have more time available for reflection, rather than reaction.

Chapter 8
Dance to the Rhythm of Meetings

*"The most important thing in communication is
to hear what is not being said."*
– Peter Drucker, Management Philosopher

Meetings often get a bad reputation – and sometimes, rightly so. Bloated agendas, unclear objectives, inconsistent formats and the nagging sense that time could have been better spent elsewhere are all too common. In high-performing organisations, meetings are not a distraction from the real work – they are how the real work gets done. When thoughtfully designed and skillfully run, meetings become the rhythm section of execution: setting the tempo, reinforcing priorities and creating the regular drumbeat that moves a business forward.

This chapter argues that effective meetings hinge on two critical dimensions. First, the right cadence and content – a deliberate flow of annual, quarterly, monthly, weekly and daily touchpoints, each with a clear purpose, sharp focus and alignment to business goals. Second, and just as vital, is the quality of facilitation. Great meetings are not monologues or passive updates – they are well-facilitated forums where multiple voices contribute to identify, understand and decide. They surface disagreement, unlock insight and build shared ownership of outcomes. In this sense, facilitation is not an administrative task but a leadership discipline that shapes culture and sharpens execution.

Senior leadership teams (SLTs) play a central role in setting this rhythm and modelling what good looks like. This chapter explores the architecture of effective meetings, focusing on how to design, run and integrate them with key management systems, such as OKRs and S&OP. It also offers practical tips for building accountability, connection and momentum at every level. Whether you're wrestling with calendar overload or simply want to get more out of the meetings you already have, this is about reclaiming meetings as high-leverage moments – where leadership is practised, strategy comes to life and progress is made visible.

The Role of Meetings in Organisational Rhythm

Meetings frequently attract criticism for being unproductive or a waste of time, most often in businesses that do not know what meetings to hold or why.[1] When structured effectively and aligned with the purpose, strategy and objectives of the business, meetings are potent tools that set the pace and rhythm of operations.

A well-structured meeting cadence – incorporating annual, quarterly, monthly, weekly and daily meetings, as well as cross-functional and project-specific touchpoints – establishes a regular discipline for communication, accountability and alignment.

Every business operates within a cycle of resetting priorities, solving problems, executing tasks and reviewing progress. Meetings serve as temporal anchors within this cycle, providing predictable opportunities for teams and individuals to coordinate, reflect and realign their efforts.

A well-designed meeting rhythm:

- Reinforces the business's purpose and strategy

- Builds a culture of trust and transparency

- Facilitates collaboration across teams

- Sets expectations and routines

- Enhances visibility and accountability

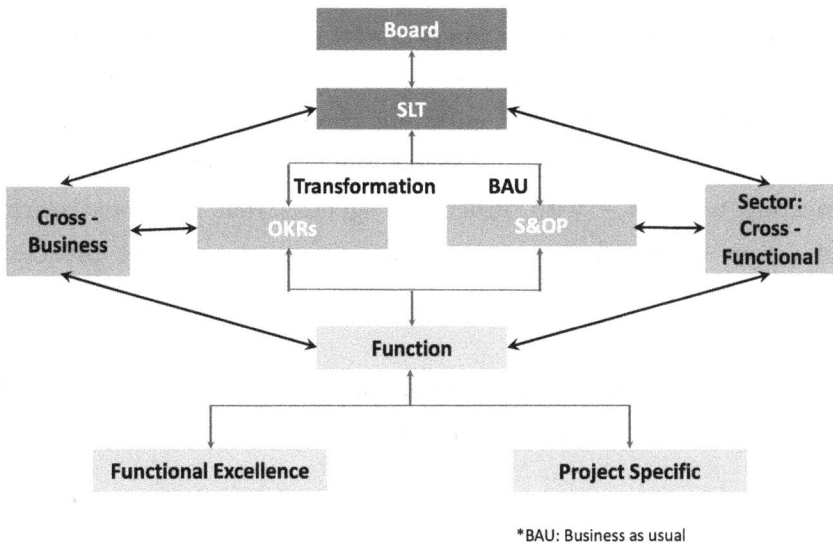

*BAU: Business as usual

Just as not all meetings are created equal, nor should their design be considered in isolation. To be effective, meetings must be clearly positioned within a broader management approach to strategy planning and execution, with defined objectives and formats that reflect the intended function of each meeting.

I recall working with a family-owned regional retail chain with 60 outlets that was struggling with inconsistent store performance and operational confusion. Senior leaders held long, irregular meetings driven by day-to-day firefighting. There was no consistent approach to surfacing store-level issues or sharing best practices. Decisions were revisited multiple times with no clear record or accountability.

As tension over operational issues reached a crisis point, the MD introduced a structured meeting framework, including weekly operations meetings, monthly performance reviews and a scorecard to track progress. Regional managers were directed to hold 30-minute weekly "huddles" with store managers. Within six months, stock accuracy improved by 25%, customer complaints decreased by 18% and employee turnover dropped by 22%. A predictable, disciplined meeting cadence – with structured agendas that promoted clarity of action – helped the business move from reactive to proactive operations.

The schematic below introduces each main meeting type and how it sets the cadence to a business's rhythm.

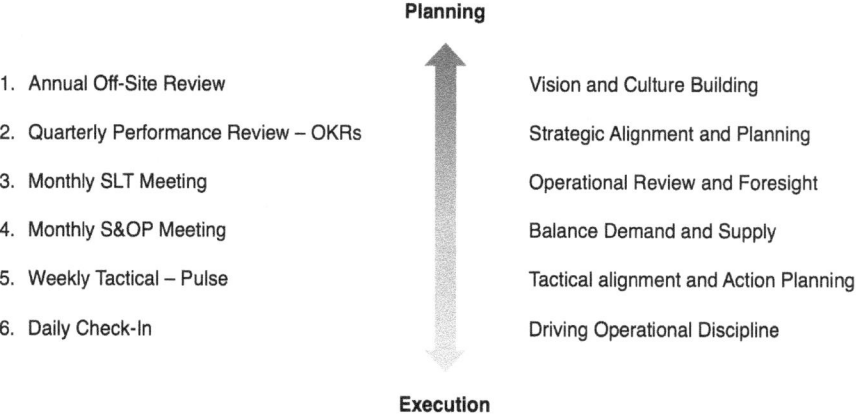

Planning

1. Annual Off-Site Review	Vision and Culture Building
2. Quarterly Performance Review – OKRs	Strategic Alignment and Planning
3. Monthly SLT Meeting	Operational Review and Foresight
4. Monthly S&OP Meeting	Balance Demand and Supply
5. Weekly Tactical – Pulse	Tactical alignment and Action Planning
6. Daily Check-In	Driving Operational Discipline

Execution

Annual Meetings: Vision and Culture Building

Purpose:

Annual meetings serve as strategic reset points. These meetings focus on vision, culture, long-term planning and leadership alignment. They typically integrate with budgeting, reforecasting and business performance reviews.

Role of SLT Leaders:

At strategy off-sites, SLT leaders lead the conversation on vision, market trends, opportunities and key strategic decisions. They don't just present slides or nod along to whatever the MD suggests. They challenge assumptions, clarify the company's "why" and ensure every strategic direction is grounded in customer insight, capability and financial reality. They do so to build ownership of the outcomes. Without constructive conflict and debate, what emerges from these sessions is invariably lightweight and lacks substantive commitment to action.

Typical format:

One or more days, often offsite.

Key themes:

- Review of the year's performance and lessons learned

- Revisiting vision, mission and values

- Strategic planning and target setting for the coming year

- Leadership development and cultural initiatives

Pros:

- Aligns the organisation at the highest level

- Re-energises the SLT around purpose and strategy

- Supports succession planning and culture shaping

- Encourages deep reflection and breakthrough thinking

Cons:

- Expensive and time-consuming

- Can feel overly aspirational without clear follow-through

- Risks of being disconnected from front-line reality

Best use:
Strategy off-sites are foundational events that reinforce purpose, values and long-term priorities. The most effective off-sites are retreats where the SLT invests time to bond at a deeper level through shared activities or structured learning – e.g. inviting an external speaker on leadership, team development, personal productivity or well-being. Even investing just half a day in this way can shift the mood, unlock fresh perspectives and deepen connection.

Quarterly Meetings: Strategic Alignment and Planning

Purpose:

Quarterly meetings set the tempo for strategic execution. They are designed to evaluate progress toward longer-term goals, set new quarterly OKRs, assess market changes and refine priorities.

Role of SLT Leaders:

In quarterly OKR reviews, SLT leaders ensure that what the business said it would do is being actively measured, evaluated and learned from. These meetings aren't about finger-pointing or showboating – they are about creating learning loops and building accountability. SLT leaders reinforce that OKRs are not tasks – they are results that matter. By being well-prepared, curious and engaged, they turn OKR reviews into energising checkpoints that sharpen focus and drive alignment.

Typical format:

Half- to full-day workshops or off-sites.

Key elements include:

- Review of last quarter's OKRs and results

- Market and customer insights

- Capability development assessments

- Setting new OKRs and key initiatives

Pros:

- Creates space for high-level thinking

- Aligns the SLT and key managers around short-term strategic priorities

- Reinforces long-term vision and purpose

- Facilitates cross-functional coordination

Cons:

- Time-intensive and logistically complex

- Requires strong facilitation and preparation

- Can feel disconnected from daily operations if not grounded in reality

Best use:
SLT, cross-functional strategy groups and project leaders use quarterly meetings to ensure the execution of the strategy is set up to succeed, align priorities and communicate direction. These meetings are essential for OKR planning, as they set the management agenda and focus for the following three months.

Monthly SLT Meetings: Operational Review and Foresight

Purpose:
Monthly meetings provide a broader view than weekly sessions. They focus on trends, performance analysis and medium-term planning. These meetings often serve as a forum for SLT leaders to understand how various functions are performing in relation to strategic targets, and to collaborate on addressing specific challenges.

Role of SLT Leaders:
These meetings are where execution risk meets interdependence. SLT leaders ensure departments are not rowing in different directions but are sharing key information, raising risks and providing support. By encouraging transparency, respectful debate and shared accountability, SLT leaders help build a leadership culture that is collaborative rather than siloed. When well chaired, these meetings act as the nerve centre of operational leadership.

Typical format:
2 to 3 hours

Structured agendas often include:

- Financial or operational dashboards

- Review of performance against OKRs

- Risk or opportunity analysis

- Resolution of development issues or challenges

- Medium-term resource planning

Pros:

- Bridges the gap between short-term execution and long-term strategy

- Supports early identification of course corrections

Cons:

- Risk of duplication with weekly meetings if not clearly scoped

- Time-consuming if not facilitated efficiently

- May encourage over-analysis at the expense of decisive action

Best use:
For SLT and cross-functional teams responsible for delivery, monthly meetings are ideal for surfacing strategic issues and refining tactical approaches. They should be structured to allow for concise reporting on OKRs and KPIs, followed by in-depth analysis of challenges that may be hindering the business and require attention.

Monthly S&OP: Balance Demand and Supply

Purpose:
The S&OP meeting is a strategic, cross-functional meeting that aligns sales, marketing, supply chain, finance and operations around a single, agreed plan for the medium to long term (usually 3–18 months). Its core objective is to balance demand and supply, ensure resource

availability and align operating plans with the company's financial goals and strategic objectives.

This meeting is designed for:

- Forecasting demand more accurately

- Aligning supply plans to demand realities

- Resolving trade-offs across functions, e.g. sales targets vs. production capacity

- Driving consensus on key decisions affecting customers, products and profitability

- Improving business performance predictability

Role of SLT Leaders:

S&OP meetings require trade-offs between ambition and reality: sales versus capacity, margin versus market share, and investment versus cash flow. SLT leaders bring strategic priorities into these decisions, helping teams make more aligned choices. Their participation transforms the S&OP from a cross-department review into a more controlled strategic process – linking operational data directly to company goals.

Typical format:

1 to 2 hours

Preparation work:

- Data collection and validation, such as sales forecasts, inventory levels, backlog, supply constraints and financial projections

- Functional reviews such as demand planning, supply planning and financial modelling

Agenda:

- Review of previous month's performance: variances of actual vs. forecast, sales, inventory, production and achieved margins

- Demand review: updated sales forecasts, promotion planning, market insights

- Supply review: capacity plans, inventory analysis, production constraints, logistics challenges

- Financial review: impact of plans on revenue, margin and working capital

- Risk and opportunity: scenario planning – upside/downside analysis

- Executive decisions: key decisions documented with ownership and next steps

Pros:

- Breaks down silos between departments and builds a unified business plan

- Improves forecast accuracy

- Helps foresee and manage supply–demand mismatches and external risks

- Provides a clear line of sight across operational, financial and commercial domains

- Encourages scenario planning and well-informed trade-offs

Cons:

- Requires rigorous data collection, preparation and coordination across teams

- Poor inputs (e.g. inaccurate forecasts) lead to poor decisions with "garbage in, garbage out" consequences

- Without top-level SLT support, decisions may not be actioned, risking duplication or overlap with monthly meetings

- Teams used to working in silos may resist the transparency and alignment required

Best use:
The S&OP meeting integrates strategic planning with operational execution, driving accountability for forecast accuracy and operational readiness. Data requirements and quality preparation suggest the S&OP process is best suited as a monthly meeting to balance demand and supply in a dynamic business environment. However, in times of stress, meeting frequency can be increased.

Integrating S&OP with OKRs is a crucial step in ensuring that operational planning is aligned with strategic goals. If OKRs set intent, S&OP brings feasibility to the delivery plan. OKRs are refreshed quarterly, but many require long-range operational alignment, which S&OP provides. S&OP tends to identify capacity constraints, risks or new opportunities, which then feed back into and improve OKR planning.

OKRs can be integrated into the S&OP cycle by using them to frame discussions, starting each cycle with a review of current OKRs:

In the **demand review**, link forecasts to growth-related OKRs.

In the **supply review**, connect supply and operational KPIs to cost or margin OKRs.

In the **financial review**, map P&L and cash flow implications back to strategic outcomes.

In the **risk and opportunity discussion**, prioritise actions with the highest leverage against OKRs.

When S&OP and OKRs are run in isolation, there is a risk of strategy without execution (OKRs that don't get delivered) or execution without strategy (S&OP plans that are efficient but misaligned). When fully integrated, OKRs give meaning to the S&OP process, and S&OP provides the muscle to bring OKRs to life. Together, they bridge the gap between ambition and action.

From OKRs to S&OP	From S&OP to OKRs
Define the "why" behind supply/demand	Highlight constraints or opportunities
Prioritise what needs to be enabled	Adjust objectives or key results based on the new reality
Set financial expectations	Update forecasts and delivery plans

The two-way feedback loop helps the business stay agile, strategic and realistic, so that planning is not just about forecasting, but also about orchestrating outcomes.

Integrating S&OP with OKRs

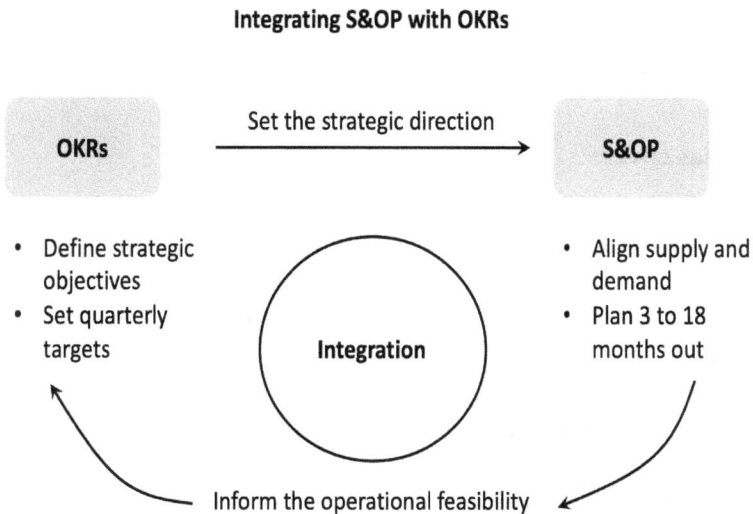

Weekly Meetings: Tactical Alignment

Purpose:
Weekly meetings allow SLT leaders and managers to review current trading performance, address issues and adjust tactics. They focus on execution, short-term resource allocation and action planning.

Role of SLT Leaders:
Weekly meetings are where tactics meet time pressure. SLT leaders do not dominate; instead, they support, unblock and reinforce speed and clarity by modelling brevity and results-focused dialogue. By treating the weekly meeting as critical, the SLT strengthens the importance of disciplined execution and helps keep teams energised and focused on progress, not perfection.

Typical format:
30 to 60 minutes, once a week at the start of the week.

Agendas cover:

- Customer and staff news

- Summary review of KPIs (Scorecard) and on/off-track check-in on OKRs

- New business priorities

- Tactical challenges and solutions

- Adjustments to plans or resources

- Communication of actions from the meeting

Pros:

- Sets a fast, businesslike pace for the working week and confirms accountability

- Encourages participation and shared problem-solving

- Provides updates across the business and keeps everybody on track

- Can be used to reinforce values and celebrate wins

Cons:

- Can become bloated with too many agenda items

- Risk of micromanagement if improperly scoped

- May become more of a report-out than a working session

Best use:
SLT and cross-functional leadership teams benefit from weekly meetings to keep strategy execution on track. They are also ideal for reinforcing progress toward OKRs by identifying obstacles that need to be overcome.

I recently partnered with a mid-size SaaS business employing 120 staff that was experiencing rapid growth but suffered from disjointed execution. SLT meetings were ad hoc and without agendas. Department heads operated in silos, with little understanding of each other's priorities. Product delays, rework and duplicated efforts were common. Team frustrations were high, especially over unclear decisions and shifting priorities.

The business adopted a rhythm of weekly tactical meetings using the EOS Level 10 format[2], supplemented by monthly cross-functional reviews and quarterly off-sites. Clear agendas, pre-read expectations and decision logs were implemented. Within two quarters, the business reduced product delivery cycle time by 30%, increased inter-departmental engagement scores and launched three key initiatives ahead of schedule. The new meeting structure, with its emphasis on the weekly Level 10 meeting, built confidence. Supporting meetings brought fewer surprises, stronger execution and more effective cross-functional alignment.

Weekly meetings are tactically oriented sessions. Often, the most practical step one can take is to design issue-based meetings to run alongside the weekly meeting, bringing together the most relevant and knowledgeable people to identify the root cause of a challenge and create an action plan. Weekly meetings cannot, and should not, become the venue for addressing all issues. If a particular meeting starts to assume this behavioural characteristic, it is a sign that the meeting discipline is drifting off track.

Daily Meetings: Driving Operational Discipline

Purpose:
Daily meetings, often referred to as stand-ups or huddles, are brief check-ins to align a team on immediate priorities, identify blockers and coordinate efforts.

Role of SLT Leaders:

They don't need to attend every daily stand-up. Still, when they do, SLT leaders humanise leadership and signal that small actions matter – for example, by offering a brief reminder of a key priority, sharing a customer insight or expressing gratitude for yesterday's wins. When SLT leaders attend, they listen more than they speak, to learn what is really going on and to model behaviours such as accountability, humility and urgency. Even a brief appearance by an SLT leader can lift energy and reinforce priorities. It sends the message: "Leadership is in the trenches with you."

Typical format:

10 to 15 minutes, same time every day.

Each team member shares:

- What they did yesterday

- What they plan to do today

- Any obstacles they are facing

Pros:

- Promotes clarity and focus

- Enhances communication within teams

- Encourages quick identification of issues

- Builds a habit of daily accountability

Cons:

- Can become rote or redundant without purposeful facilitation

- Risks turning into status updates rather than problem-solving sessions

- Not always useful for more senior staff with less day-to-day detail

Best use:
Operational teams, such as sales, customer service and development teams, benefit most from daily huddles. They work best when closely linked to immediate priorities or short-term targets.

Design Meetings to Add Value

The true value of meetings comes not just from their frequency or structure but from their alignment. Meetings that are clearly positioned within the context of the company's purpose, strategy and OKRs become more than administrative events – they become instruments of transformation. Meetings can be the engine room of great organisations, or the biggest drag on time and morale. The difference lies not in the type or frequency of meetings, but in their design, facilitation and alignment. When meetings are purposeful, focused and actionable, people show up not just out of obligation, but because they receive value, feel accountable and are inspired to contribute.

Aligning with purpose. When meetings explicitly reinforce the organisation's core purpose, they serve as cultural touchstones.

The SLT can use recurring meetings to communicate values, share impact stories and remind teams why their work matters. This emotional connection improves engagement and morale.

Anchoring to strategic goals. Meetings that are rooted in strategic priorities avoid the trap of busywork. Reviewing initiatives in terms of their strategic impact rather than activity prevents drift and keeps teams focused on what truly matters.

Connecting to OKRs. OKRs translate strategy into actionable objectives. Embedding OKR review and tracking into meeting agendas ensures a rhythm of accountability. Daily and weekly meetings track key results, while monthly meetings evaluate progress. Quarterly sessions set new objectives, and annual meetings align OKRs with the broader mission.

When OKRs are present in meetings:

- Teams see how their work contributes to bigger goals

- Leaders have a structured way to assess progress

- Priorities can be adapted quickly based on results

A well-crafted meeting cadence is like a company's heartbeat. It keeps the business alive, in sync and moving forward. By transforming meetings from isolated events into components of a deliberate operating rhythm, SLTs can improve communication, accelerate progress and achieve their goals with greater focus and cohesion.

The best meetings accomplish real work. When people learn that meetings actually accomplish something, they stop making excuses to be elsewhere. I was once engaged by a 30-person creative agency that gave off the happy impression of being highly collaborative, but below the surface, the reality was chaos. Constant deadline pressures, last-minute rushes, missed briefs and frustrated clients were commonplace. Project teams were self-organising and lacked formal check-ins. The creative and account teams frequently clashed over scope creep and timelines.

We quickly introduced daily stand-ups, weekly project reviews and bi-weekly client alignment meetings. Agendas and time-boxed discussions helped maintain energy and improve clarity of focus. Over a three-month period, client satisfaction scores increased by 52%, and project rework was reduced by 40%. All teams benefit from structure – provided it respects their culture and pace.

The most effective SLT leaders understand that strategy doesn't live in slide decks. It thrives in moments of shared decision-making, cross-functional alignment and frontline pressures. By showing up fully, asking the right questions and reinforcing the right behaviours in every type of meeting, they become architects of clarity and catalysts of execution. Ultimately, it's not just what SLT leaders say in meetings, it's how they show up that determines how the organisation follows through.

One classic example of dysfunctional meetings is the chronic inability to make timely decisions. Issues that should be resolved in the moment get passed up the chain in an endless cycle of deferral. Daily operational matters are bumped to weekly meetings, which are then postponed to monthly reviews and so on – until what started as a manageable question ends up clogging the agenda of a quarterly or even annual discussion. The result is a sluggish, risk-averse culture where momentum stalls, problems fester and accountability becomes diluted.[3]

At the heart of this dysfunction is a failure to empower people to act (see Chapter 4, *"Delegate Authority to Empower and Create Leaders"*) and a failure of meetings to fulfil their intended purpose. When every decision requires escalation, meetings become bottlenecks rather than enablers of progress. The SLT has a critical role to play in breaking this cycle – not just by speeding things up, but by setting the expectation that decisions must be made at the right level, by the right people, at the right time. That means drawing a line: "We cannot escalate this matter – this team must take a position now. What is our view?"[4]

This shift requires courage, clarity and commitment from the SLT. It also demands that meetings are facilitated in a way that enables decisions – not just reports, opinions or updates. This includes defining clear decision rights, using creative problem-solving frameworks to test trade-offs, and developing a culture where people feel safe to challenge and commit. When SLTs lead in this way, meetings stop being a theatre of avoidance and become engines of resolution – places where the business gets unstuck and moves forward with purpose.

Summary

Meetings play a vital role in establishing a regular operating rhythm – or "drumbeat" – that drives focus, alignment and accountability across the business. Far from being a distraction, the right meetings, when designed and facilitated well, become a powerful lever for execution. Their impact hinges on two essential dimensions: the cadence and agenda, as well as the quality of facilitation.

Cadence ensures the right conversations occur at the right frequency, aligned with the business's needs. Each meeting type serves a distinct purpose:

Annual strategy meetings. Set long-term direction and define high-level goals.

Quarterly OKR meetings. Translate strategy into measurable outcomes and align execution.

Monthly SLT meetings. Focus on business performance, cross-functional coordination and resolving strategic challenges and issues

S&OP meetings. Ensure supply, demand and resources are balanced to support delivery and growth.

Weekly tactical meetings. Drive short-term execution, resolve roadblocks and track metrics.

Daily stand-ups. Support rapid communication, coordination and team cohesion at the front line.

But cadence alone isn't enough. What brings meetings to life is strong facilitation – the ability to structure discussion so that multiple voices are heard, real understanding is built and informed decisions are made. Effective facilitation encourages people to move beyond updates and opinions, to collectively identify, understand and decide on what matters most.

Together, these two dimensions – meeting architecture and facilitation quality – create a deliberate rhythm that helps organisations stay agile, aligned and execution-focused. When meetings are run well, they stop being something to endure and become the place where leadership is practised and progress is made.

Reflective Questions

The questions set out below are designed to help you internalise key ideas, examine your own experiences in light of what you've read, and consider how any insights might shape your thinking and actions in future. There are no right answers, only honest ones. Use these opportunities to reflect to deepen your awareness, spark conversation with others or simply increase awareness of what's changing for you as you make progress through this book.

Are our top-level strategic priorities visible in every major meeting?

Do all recurring meetings have a defined owner, purpose and success metric?

Are OKRs reviewed with a clear cadence and tied to actions across levels?

Do meetings enable fast, confident decisions, not just discussions?

Do teams know what to expect and how to prepare for each type of meeting?

Is our meeting calendar a reflection of our strategy, not just our habits?

Is our calendar a reflection of our strategy, not just our habits? There is a longer list of questions in the "Appendix: Reflective Questions." These are designed to be addressed when you, with or without the team, have more time available for reflection, rather than reaction.

Chapter 9
Raising the Bar with 1-2-1s

"When it comes to motivation, there's a gap between what science knows and what business does. For 21st-century work, we need to upgrade away from carrots and sticks, and towards autonomy, mastery and purpose."
– Daniel H. Pink, Author

In the rhythm of working life – filled with strategy meetings, project updates and impromptu catch-ups – there is one meeting that holds more potential than any other to influence outcomes, nurture talent and shape culture: the 1-2-1 meeting between a senior leadership team (SLT) member and a direct report. When done well, this conversation is not just a recurring calendar entry – it is the most important, intimate and impactful conversation in the working month. This chapter explores how senior leaders can turn 1-2-1s from routine meetings into high-impact leadership tools.

A 1-2-1 is deeply personal. It creates space for honest reflection, focused feedback and purposeful dialogue. It shifts attention from urgent tasks to long-term growth and alignment, allowing leaders to surface challenges, celebrate wins and coach individuals towards their potential. When leaders show up consistently, listen actively and tailor their approach, they send a powerful message: "You matter. Your growth matters. And I'm here to help you succeed."

This chapter lays out the practical foundations of great 1-2-1s: how to structure them, how to integrate them into performance systems and how to handle even the toughest conversations with care and clarity. From the GROW coaching model to the principles of Radical Candour, it equips leaders with tools to foster accountability and motivation. More than a management practice, 1-2-1s are a relational discipline – and when taken seriously, they raise the bar for leadership across the business.

The Underrated Superpower of the 1-2-1

Unlike team meetings, the 1-2-1 is designed with one person in mind. It is their time, and the focus is on them receiving feedback and taking ownership of the situation. It is personal, reflective and relational – and that is precisely what makes it so powerful. In a working world focused on output, targets and efficiency, the 1-2-1 stands apart as a space where the human element of work breathes, and where listening, honesty, vulnerability and encouragement can thrive.

A great 1-2-1 can change working patterns and relationships. It shifts focus from what is urgent to what is important. It uncovers what is unsaid and provides the psychological safety for people to speak candidly, surface challenges and share ideas without fear of judgment. Done regularly and with intention, these conversations build trust, foster connection and unlock performance.

At its heart, a 1-2-1 is a relational ritual. It is a moment when a manager can say, not with words but with presence and the commitment of time, "You matter to me." That message resonates deeply, particularly in environments where people may feel as if they are just cogs in a machine. When a team member experiences that kind of attention, it strengthens their sense of belonging – and with belonging comes engagement, discretionary effort and loyalty.

This connection matters not only for morale but also for building a collaborative spirit. People who feel seen and heard by their managers are more likely to share openly, ask for help, take risks and lean into their development. The 1-2-1 is key to how SLT leaders build influence through consistent, authentic connection and how they recognise when a simple invitation to a team member in a meeting to share their view will lead to the most valuable insights.

Done well, 1-2-1s create clarity. For the employee, it can be a mirror reflecting their progress, challenges and growth. For the SLT leader, it can be a window into the reality of what is happening on the ground. Too often, leaders rely on dashboards, reports or group meetings to understand what is happening. But data alone does not tell the whole story. In 1-2-1s, leaders can uncover the context behind the numbers, including missed opportunities, friction between teams, or personal struggles that are affecting performance. It is where real-time intelligence lives "off the record" and beneath the surface.

Moreover, it is where the narrative of work gets shaped. In the absence of a good 1-2-1, staff are left to write their own stories – often filled with assumptions, frustrations and doubts. By sharing time in private, leaders and team members can co-author a different story – one of progress, purpose and partnership. The structure of most organisations prioritises performance and productivity, but a 1-2-1 meeting allows space to discuss the person behind the performance.

Questions such as:

- How are you feeling?

- What issues are not being resolved?

- What are you proud of that no one has noticed?

- What experience and skills do you want to develop?

When an SLT leader makes time for these kinds of questions, it sends a powerful signal: *You're not just a resource. I care about your whole experience here.* When employees feel that, they begin to show up differently. They bring more of themselves to work. They take ownership of their growth. They start to trust the system – and the person leading them. These conversations act as pressure valves, allowing people to release tension before it boils over. They prevent minor issues from becoming big problems and create opportunities for repair and recalibration long before resentment takes root.

Great 1-2-1s do not just maintain connections – they accelerate development. SLT leaders who use these meetings to coach, challenge and champion their people become powerful catalysts for growth. The 1-2-1 becomes a dynamic, agile space for learning. Goals can be refined, feedback provided in the moment and development plans can evolve organically. It is where career aspirations can be explored, blind spots can be uncovered and ambitions can be aligned with business needs. Approached in this way, the 1-2-1 becomes more than a check-in – it becomes a checkpoint on the journey to professional maturity, moving people from being managed to being mentored. High performance does not happen by accident – it is cultivated. And 1-2-

1s are one of the most reliable mediums for delivering transformation in performance.

Through regular, meaningful conversations, leaders can align expectations, course-correct in real time and give praise that lands because it is personal and specific. 1-2-1s support clarity in action. Employees thrive when they know what is expected of them, how they are doing and where they are going. A great 1-2-1 delivers all three. It ensures that goals are understood, blockers are addressed and recognition is timely. And when performance dips, it is the foundation of trust built in 1-2-1s that allows for honest, constructive feedback without damaging morale.

Of all the interactions in a leader's calendar, none hold more potential than the 1-2-1 with direct reports. It is the lever that can move both hearts and minds. It is where culture is lived, not just talked about. It is where alignment happens – not just with strategy but with values. When SLT leaders prioritise these meetings, they send a powerful message to their teams: *You matter. Your voice matters. Your growth matters.* In return, they gain loyalty, engagement and insight.

To make 1-2-1s truly impactful, they must be intentional. For leaders, that means:

Consistency. Don't cancel them. Show up every time – it builds trust.

Preparation. Come with questions, not just updates. Think about what the other person might need.

Presence. Unless you are connecting remotely, please put your laptop and mobile phone away. Be fully there. Listen deeply.

Personalisation. Every person is different. Tailor your approach

Follow-through. Do what you say you will do. It reinforces reliability

Integrating 1-2-1s with Performance Management

Research consistently shows that business leaders and employees have mixed feelings about the traditional annual performance review. According to a study by Deloitte, 58% of executives believe that their current performance management approach does not drive either employee engagement or high performance.[1] Many employees report that annual reviews are too infrequent, overly bureaucratic and fail to accurately reflect their actual contributions. Gallup found that only 14% of employees strongly agree that performance reviews inspire them to improve.[2]

In terms of frequency, the management trend is shifting away from annual appraisals toward more regular, ongoing feedback. Adobe is a recognised case study of a business that replaced its annual review system with frequent check-ins, yielding a 30% reduction in voluntary turnover.[3] Experience and current thinking suggest dropping the annual appraisal in favour of a cycle that includes quarterly or bi-annual reviews, complemented by regular monthly one-to-one meetings. This frequency enables timely feedback, agile goal setting and faster identification of development needs. Regular feedback is generally better received by employees, who feel more supported and aligned with their goals.

Forced rankings, a system in which employees are ranked against each other along a performance curve, have also fallen out of favour. Companies such as Microsoft and GE, once poster children for the "rank and yank" approach, have long since abandoned it.[4,5] While popular in the 1980s and 1990s, experience revealed significant drawbacks. Forced rankings can demotivate employees, increase internal competition and limit collaboration. Current performance management approaches instead favour developmental feedback over comparative evaluation. Organisations are increasingly adopting models that focus on coaching, strengths-based assessment and personalised development paths. These approaches are far more conducive to building trust, enhancing performance and retaining talent.

Ultimately, employees respect and value performance management that is fair, consistent and focused on growth. When reviews are regular, collaborative and aligned with personal and organisational goals, they become powerful tools for engagement and development. The design and implementation of the performance management system is the responsibility of the SLT. The SLT is also obliged to provide managers with the training and resources needed to conduct effective performance conversations. According to a CIPD *HR Outlook* survey, around half of HR professionals believe senior business leaders lack the people management behaviours and skills needed to get the best from their people.[6] HR professionals ranked performance management and people management as the top leadership behaviours and skills required by organisations. However, of those who chose performance management, more than half (53%) said senior leaders' current skills in this area were ineffective. Similarly, 44% felt senior leaders' people management skills were ineffective.

I have worked with several clients to introduce a simple template to guide 1-2-1s for use by the MD with direct reports, as well as by the SLT with their own teams. The approach can then be cascaded further down the organisation. The meeting guide is focused and direct, centring conversations on core business objectives, behaviours and development needs. It also provides an opportunity to record and track performance each month, enabling a more specific review in the future rather than relying solely on memory.

A great 1-2-1 should begin with the person, not the agenda. Take a few minutes to check in on life outside of work – how they are feeling, what they have planned for the weekend, how the kids (or dog) are doing, whether their partner secured that new role, or how a parent's health is progressing.

These opening minutes of genuine connection are often the most valuable. They provide insight into what is happening in someone's life that may be shaping their energy, focus or stress levels at work. Personal and professional lives are not separate – they flow together.

Building this kind of relationship makes it easier to spot challenges early, support people more effectively and navigate tough conversations with trust and understanding. But it only works if it is sincere, natural and consistently nurtured – not just a warm-up act before diving into OKRs and workstreams.

The opening personal check-in creates a natural bridge into work-related topics, where coaching frameworks such as GROW (Goal, Reality, Options, Will) can be used to explore and clarify the employee's current focus, challenges and action plan.[7]

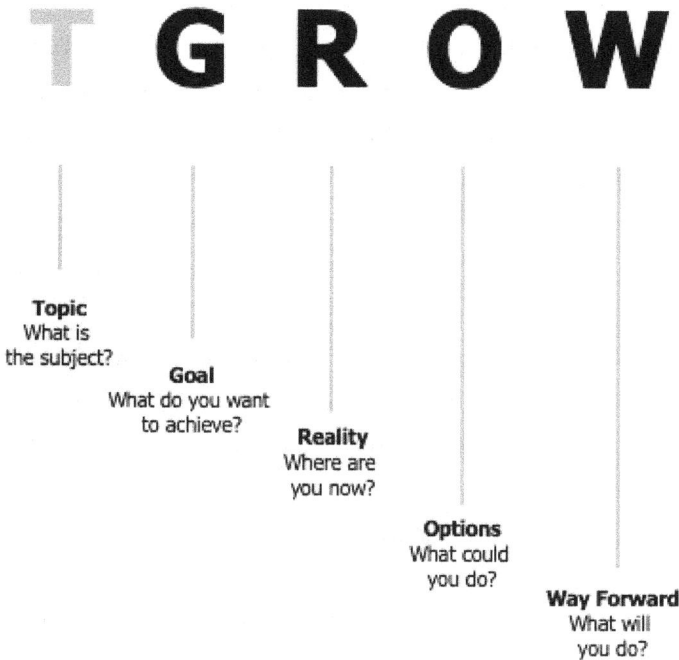

T G R O W

Topic
What is
the subject?

Goal
What do you want
to achieve?

Reality
Where are
you now?

Options
What could
you do?

Way Forward
What will
you do?

The coaching conversation starts by clarifying specific Goals, before building a better understanding of the current Reality, which identifies challenges and opportunities. Together, the manager and employee then explore possible Options or strategies for moving forward. The final stage focuses on establishing the employee's commitment – the Will – to take action and remain accountable.

The GROW model promotes self-discovery, clarifies thinking and enhances motivation, making it a highly effective tool for guiding productive, solution-focused conversations.

The 1-2-1 meeting is effective when it facilitates two-way communication between leaders and employees, allowing them to share honest expectations, progress, challenges and aspirations. A core function of the 1-2-1 is to identify areas where employees may require additional support or training. Putting development front and centre on the agenda benefits both the individual and the organisation. It also ensures that issues and development needs are addressed early and constructively, reducing the likelihood of conflict and disengagement.

When performance expectations are clear, feedback is timely and recognition is meaningful, employees are more likely to feel empowered and committed to their roles. They understand how their efforts contribute to organisational goals and are motivated to deliver their best work. Moreover, a performance-oriented culture encourages innovation and resilience. Employees are more willing to take risks, share ideas and learn from setbacks when they know that their contributions are valued and their growth is supported.

Recognition can take many forms – from verbal praise and thank-you notes to more formal awards or career progression opportunities. When integrated into the 1-2-1 cycle, recognition becomes systematic rather than sporadic, ensuring that contributions do not go unnoticed. This not only enhances employee satisfaction but also fosters a culture of excellence and accountability.

Monthly 1-2-1

Employee Name	
Month	
Team Manager	
Sickness /Absence /Late	

Objective 1	Objective 2	Objective 3
Comments (GROW)	Comments (GROW)	Comments (GROW)

Demonstration of values and behaviours this month:

What has gone well this month:

What has not gone so well this month:

Progress made on development plans:

Development of those working for you (if relevant):

Actions /Targets for 1-2-1:

EMPLOYEE ENGAGEMENT CHART			
Score 1-10 1 = 😞 10 = 😊			
Satisfied at work	Support from Manager	Knowledge of your role	Development Offered

Managers comments on your contribution?	What support can your manager provide?	Score for Month (1-10)

Employee Signature: **Date:**

219

Inevitably, individual reward becomes a talking point during 1-2-1s. When performance outcomes are linked to compensation, bonuses and other incentives, employees are more likely to be motivated to achieve and exceed expectations. However, this linkage must be transparent and based on fair, objective criteria – all too often it is not. Discretionary bonus payments should be awarded based on clear performance metrics, such as goal attainment, contribution to team success and the demonstration of organisational values.

The criteria should be communicated clearly and applied consistently to maintain credibility and trust. This not only motivates high performers but also encourages a culture based on merit, where everyone has a fair opportunity to succeed. Implemented well, the performance management system helps maintain a healthy, performance-oriented operating culture – characterised by high levels of engagement, accountability, continuous improvement and shared ownership of success.

Difficult Conversations About Performance

Addressing underperformance at the SLT level requires a delicate yet decisive approach. When an SLT leader's performance falls below expectations – or when someone in their reporting line is underperforming – the repercussions across an organisation can be felt far and wide. A well-considered and timely approach is therefore essential.

The first step is preparation. Begin by gathering objective, evidence-based data that describes the performance gap. This can include missed KPIs, feedback from stakeholders or the person's impact on team morale. Avoid anecdotal or emotionally charged evidence, as it will only undermine the integrity of the discussion. Documented data helps to keep the conversation fact-based and constructive. Timing is also crucial. While it may sometimes be necessary to show flexibility and accommodate moments of high stress or heavy workload, the meeting should take place within the established cycle of 1-2-1s.

Few business leaders will admit it, but the "shit sandwich" is one of the most popular – and least effective – ways to give feedback. Sometimes more charitably referred to as a "praise sandwich" or "compliment sandwich," this technique involves placing negative feedback neatly between two positive points. The idea is that negative feedback is more easily accepted if it is preceded by positive reinforcement. Unsurprisingly, it often has the opposite effect. Negative feedback is usually buried, vague and easily dismissed. Put another way, when you serve someone a "shit sandwich," they are inclined to walk away talking about the bread.

Kim Scott's model of *radical candour* sets out a powerful and practical approach to managing difficult conversations.[8] At the heart of radical candour is a simple yet transformative idea: To be an effective leader, you must *care personally* while also *challenging directly*. The strength of this approach in 1-2-1s is that it reframes feedback from being a source of fear or defensiveness to one of care.

When a leader shows they genuinely care not only about performance but also about the individual's growth and well-being, they build a relationship founded on psychological safety. This trust encourages team members to lower their guard, making them more receptive to constructive criticism. They come to understand that feedback is not about punishment or control but about support and development.

Radical Candour Model

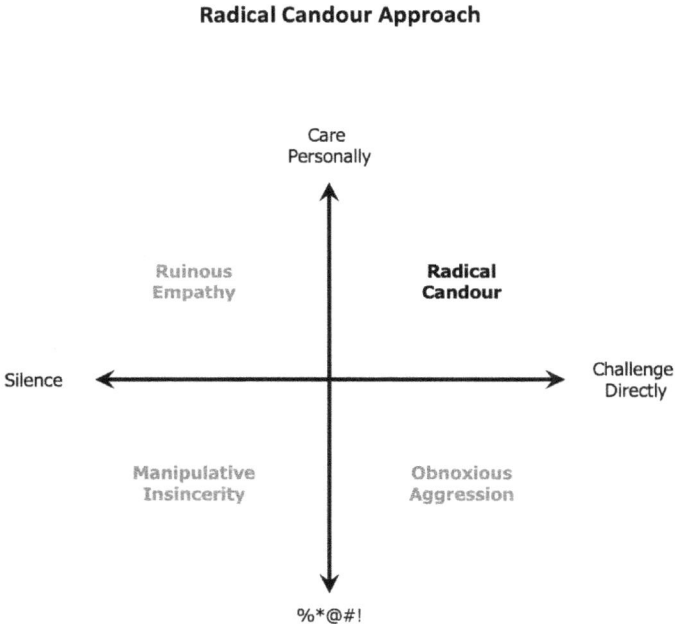

Radical Candour Approach

Care
Personally

Ruinous
Empathy

**Radical
Candour**

Silence ← → Challenge
Directly

Manipulative
Insincerity

Obnoxious
Aggression

%*@#!

Simultaneously, by challenging directly, managers avoid the pitfalls of ruinous empathy – where feedback is sugar-coated or avoided altogether to spare someone's feelings. In a radical candour-driven 1-2-1, the leader is explicit, specific and timely with feedback. This clarity helps team members understand what needs to improve and why it matters, without the confusion or resentment that vague or delayed criticism often creates.

Importantly, radical candour is not about being harsh or blunt – it is about being human and honest simultaneously. In 1-2-1 meetings, this turns a seemingly difficult conversation into an exchange that is both compassionate and productive. Team members walk away with a clear sense of what is going well, what needs to change and, most crucially, that their manager is invested in their success. The approach drives performance, deepens relationships and makes tough conversations not only easier but also more meaningful.

It is vital to set clear next steps and a follow-up plan that outlines what improvement looks like, what support is available and when progress will be reviewed.

Finally, all 1-2-1s should be documented to maintain clarity and ensure shared accountability. Records must be maintained systematically to ensure consistency, meet compliance requirements and capture what has been agreed – signed off by both parties. These records provide a valuable reference for informing future conversations, investment in development, role changes and, where necessary, disciplinary actions.

Summary

Regular, structured 1-2-1s between senior leaders and their team members are the cornerstone of effective leadership and performance management. When intentionally integrated into the rhythm of team life, these conversations become a powerful vehicle for clarity, alignment, trust and growth.

By aligning 1-2-1s with the business's performance management system, leaders can track progress on goals, surface issues early and ensure individuals are supported and challenged in equal measure. Using the GROW coaching model (Goal, Reality, Options, Will) provides a clear, repeatable structure that encourages ownership, deepens reflection and sharpens focus on outcomes. It turns each 1-2-1 into a developmental space, not just a status update.

Critically, when leaders practise radical candour – caring personally while challenging directly – they create a safe, high-trust environment for honest dialogue. This enables difficult conversations to occur with respect and purpose, tackling performance concerns, misalignment or behavioural issues early, before they escalate into deeper problems.

Over time, this disciplined and human approach to 1-2-1s builds a more engaged, accountable and high-performing culture – one conversation at a time.

Reflective Questions

The questions set out below are designed to help you internalise key ideas, examine your own experiences in light of what you've read and consider how any insights might shape your thinking and actions in future. There are no right answers – only honest ones. Use these opportunities to reflect, deepen your awareness, spark conversation with others or simply increase awareness of what is changing for you as you make progress through this book.

Are 1-2-1s viewed as a strategic leadership tool, or just a check-in over coffee?

Are 1-2-1s happening regularly and reliably, without cancelling or rescheduling?

Are 1-2-1 meetings tracking progress on goals, coaching through challenges and spotting learning opportunities?

Is there follow-through on actions or commitments made during 1-2-1s?

Is there meaningful feedback during 1-2-1s – not just praise or correction, but coaching for growth?

There is a longer list of questions in the "Appendix: Reflective Questions." These are designed to be addressed when you, with or without the team, have more time available for reflection, rather than reaction.

Chapter 10
Winning Practices and Habits

"Winning is a habit. Unfortunately, so is losing."
– Vince Lombardi, American Football Coach

Every senior leadership team (SLT) aspires to high performance, but few realise that success is less about moments of brilliance and more about the consistent application of smart, repeatable habits. Winning over time is not accidental – it is the product of rhythm, clarity and deliberate practice. This chapter explores the behaviours and routines that set exceptional SLTs apart, showing how small daily disciplines compound into significant organisational impact over time.

At the heart of this chapter is the idea that high-performing teams do not just avoid dysfunction – they cultivate a system of working that actively builds trust, sharpens focus and accelerates execution. From how meetings are run, to how resources are flexed, to how teams manage time and tension, these practices help SLTs navigate complexity with confidence. They are not about adding more work, but about working more intentionally and with purpose.

This chapter unpacks five common sources of friction that often derail senior teams – misalignment, role confusion, power dynamics, poor communication and cultural mismatch – and shows how each can be transformed into a lever for improvement. It also introduces the concept of *team flow*: that sweet spot where collaboration, clarity and momentum converge. Through a blend of practical tools and lived experience, this chapter provides a blueprint for embedding winning habits that transform potential into performance on a weekly basis.

The 5 Conflict Zones

SLTs are prone to conflict. Not all conflict is negative. Conflict can sharpen strategic focus and drive innovation, but when left to its own devices and unmanaged, it can erode trust, slow decision-making and ultimately damage organisational performance. Conflict is inevitable, and effective senior teams manage it consciously rather than reactively.

Research carried out by the CIPD shows that conflict is a significant part of workplace life, with 35% of employees experiencing some form of interpersonal conflict over the past year.[1] Common psychological or behavioural consequences included stress (48%), a drop in motivation (40%) and reduced commitment (36%), with women more likely to report these impacts. Long-term effects included low confidence and anxiety.

ACAS goes further, estimating the cost of workplace conflict in the UK at £28.5 billion (as of 2021).[2] Regardless of one's opinion on the accuracy of such projections, conflict resolution remains a core leadership skill. As Dwight Eisenhower, 34th President of the USA and five-star general during WW2, once put it: *"You don't lead by hitting people over the head – that's assault, not leadership."*

Research on this topic – supported by first-hand experience – consistently shows that conflict within SLTs tends to cluster around five key issues:[3-5]

1. Strategic direction and priorities

2. Role clarity and accountability

3. Power dynamics and influence

4. Communication and information sharing

5. Personal values and leadership style

Let's go a little deeper on each of these in turn.

Strategic Direction and Priorities

The most common flashpoint for SLT conflict is disagreement over the organisation's strategic direction and priorities. Each SLT leader typically brings a distinct perspective based on their area of expertise, such as finance, operations, marketing, people or technology. While this diversity is valuable, it can lead to different interpretations of what success looks like and how it can be best achieved.

Conflicts often arise when strategic goals are vague, competing or not transparently prioritised. Consequently, leaders may find themselves advocating for their department's shorter-term needs, which can lead to tension when resource allocation decisions favour one area over another. Moreover, when external conditions change – such as market disruption or regulatory change – SLTs that lack clear, aligned strategic thinking struggle to adapt cohesively, as each person uses their own frame of reference to evaluate the shifting dynamics.

Healthy SLTs enjoy open debates about strategy and ultimately converge on clear, agreed priorities. Without this, execution suffers and the organisation risks becoming increasingly short-term in outlook and pulling itself apart from the top. Refer to Chapter 6 for a step-by-step guide on addressing the root cause by developing a strategic action plan that can be effectively executed.

Role Clarity and Accountability

Another major source of conflict is confusion over roles and responsibilities. Senior teams often suffer from what may best be called a *grey zone* – where ownership of key initiatives or decisions is unclear. Sometimes, job titles can create confusion if they are poorly defined or inconsistently interpreted across the organisation. The lack of clarity can cause frustration, either through overlaps that lead to duplicated effort or accountability gaps where critical work falls through "the cracks." Whatever the reason, accountability becomes blurred. The knock-on behaviours are that leaders may deflect blame when outcomes are poor, or reach into others' domains when boundaries are not respected.

When each member of the leadership team knows where their authority begins and ends, conflict decreases and collaboration becomes easier and more natural. There is no substitute for taking the time to document formal job descriptions and to clarify decision-making processes – for example, in the form of a RACI matrix – that provide direction on how core business processes are managed. High-performing SLTs go beyond documents by respecting expertise and ownership, ensuring a seamless workflow. Put simply, this means trusting colleagues to own their space and holding back from stepping into each other's remits unless explicitly invited.

See Chapter 5 for a profile of the types of underlying organisational issues that are best addressed explicitly and collectively, to clarify key operating principles for SLT leaders.

Power Dynamics and Influence

Even in well-functioning teams, issues of power and influence are present. Conflict often emerges when individuals feel sidelined, undermined or unfairly dominated by others.[6] Senior leaders often have strong egos – after all, they are used to leading large teams or departments. Navigating shared leadership and concepts such as *collective cabinet responsibility* requires a level of humility and trust that can be challenging to sustain. Unacknowledged power struggles may manifest subtly, through passive resistance, exclusion from key conversations or lobbying for support outside formal meetings. They may also appear more overtly in open clashes during executive meetings or as hardened factions within the team.

I recall that shortly after my first Board appointment – which initially felt like a time for celebration – I was taken aside by a colleague with 30 years more service on the Board than I. He wanted to make it very clear that I was "only a junior director." At one level, I "got it," but it was hardly welcoming, and certainly not the foundation I had expected after accepting the legal responsibilities of becoming a director. In short, it put me "on guard."

It is far healthier to acknowledge the natural existence of influence and to distribute decision-making power based on expertise – not skewed by something less relevant, such as length of service or family relationships. Refer to Chapter 2 for guidance on steps to consider when establishing foundational alignment.

Communication and Information Sharing

Breakdowns in communication are a universal cause of team dysfunction, but at the SLT level, the stakes are particularly high. Information asymmetry – where some leaders are better informed than others – can breed suspicion, mistrust and resentment. Poor communication practices can also lead to misunderstandings, wasted effort or misaligned messaging with colleagues, customers and suppliers.

Key communication breakdowns often include:

- Withholding information to maintain an advantage

- Failing to actively listen or check for understanding

- Speaking in vague or ambiguous ways

- Assuming alignment without verifying it

Effective communication within a senior leadership team requires more than good intentions. It demands deliberate, structured practices. This includes regular updates, open feedback channels and the willingness to surface and explore differing assumptions. It also calls for emotional intelligence: the ability to listen deeply, read between the lines and speak with clarity, candour and respect.

Too often, it is assumed that everyone at the SLT level is a natural communicator who will instinctively share relevant information to keep colleagues informed and aligned. Yet under pressure, when stress and workload increase, communication is often the first thing to fall away. It is wrongly perceived as a "nice to have" or "soft stuff" when in fact it is essential to cohesion and performance.

Not every leader has the same instinct or style when it comes to communication. Some are naturally expressive and transparent, while others struggle to keep up with email, remain visible or proactively share updates.[7] Such variation is why communication should never be left to chance or personality. It needs to be a shared expectation – embedded into the culture and consistently role-modelled by the SLT.

During periods of high workload, open and consistent communication becomes even more critical. It ensures that inevitable tensions or conflicts remain constructive rather than turning corrosive. For more on the rhythm of communication that keeps teams aligned and coordinated, see Chapter 8, which discusses the essential meetings that help people move together in an informed, disciplined formation.

Personal Values and Leadership Style

Ultimately, conflict often arises from differences in personal values or leadership styles. While strategic or operational conflicts can usually be solved with logic and process, clashes over fundamental beliefs about leadership, ethics or culture are much harder to navigate.

A leader who believes deeply in rapid, decisive action may find themselves at odds with a colleague who values careful, time-consuming consensus building. One leader might prioritise aggressive growth, while another places emphasis on risk management and sustainability. These value-based differences can create tensions that affect every strategic discussion and operational decision. Leadership style mismatches also matter. One leader's coaching approach may clash with another's more authoritative, command-and-control style. On its own, this is not necessarily an issue, but it can make cross-functional collaboration painful and difficult.

High-performing SLTs do not seek to homogenise values or standardise styles. Instead, they bring these differences to the surface, respect them and find ways to bridge them when required. Teams that can name and discuss value differences without judgment are the ones built to last. See Chapter 1 for context on understanding individual motivations, and Chapter 9 for guidance on tapping into and aligning the capacity to contribute.

Conflict in senior leadership teams is inevitable and, in many cases, desirable. It reflects the reality that complex organisations require diverse perspectives and passionate debate in the face of competing priorities. However, when conflict stems from persistent misalignment on strategy, unclear roles, unhealthy power dynamics, poor communication or incompatible values and styles, it can paralyse decision-making and damage organisational health.

By understanding these five common sources of conflict and addressing them directly, SLTs can transform conflict from a threat into a catalyst for stronger collaboration, faster execution and greater impact. The path forward lies not in eliminating conflict, but in managing it wisely – with courage and emotional intelligence. Which of the five sources of conflict most affects your SLT, and how will you address it? Ironically, it is by understanding the causes of conflict that leaders can create the template for building a high-performing SLT.

Addressing the five sources of conflict sets the environment and conditions for achieving *team flow* – by putting in place the supporting structures, processes and behavioural expectations. By naming and addressing hidden tensions, friction is reduced and psychological safety is increased. This clarity frees up energy previously lost to mistrust, confusion or power struggles, and encourages leaders to focus on shared goals with confidence and momentum. When roles, values and communication norms are aligned, collaboration occurs with ease, decisions move more quickly and innovation unfolds more naturally.

Team flow emerges not by accident, but by intentionally creating the environmental conditions where trust, clarity and mutual accountability thrive.

Team Flow

The concept of *flow*, first introduced by psychologist Mihaly Csikszentmihalyi, describes a mental state in which a person becomes fully immersed in an activity, experiencing energised focus, deep involvement and genuine enjoyment.[8] In flow, action and awareness merge to the extent that time often seems to fly by, and self-consciousness diminishes. While the idea was initially associated with individual pursuits – such as athletics, the arts and craftsmanship – flow is increasingly being explored in the context of teams, particularly

SLTs, where the stakes are high, complexity is great and seamless collaboration is critical.

For SLTs, achieving a collective state of flow can unlock extraordinary levels of performance. When in flow, teams make better decisions, communicate with less friction and operate with a shared sense of purpose. The strategic, operational and cultural benefits are profound. However, accessing this state – and sustaining it – requires deliberate structure and effort.

Flow at the team level is not simply the sum of individual flow experiences. It is a shared dynamic in which the group operates as a coherent unit, navigating challenges in a synchronised, intuitive way. You often recognise team flow when meetings are deeply engaging rather than draining; when ideas build naturally on one another; when disagreements fuel creativity instead of conflict; and when outcomes consistently exceed expectations.

I recall periods of being in team flow with colleagues where we all instinctively knew what we were each doing, without needing to explain in detail. We just acted – mainly because we had faced similar challenges in the past, trusted in the process and in each other and had no hesitation calling for help if confronted with something we did not understand. Together, we explored ways to make the most of our individual contributions. As a team, we intuitively unified, thinking about how we could help each other achieve more. It is when this shift of attention – intentionally from self to others – is made that you recognise you are working in the flow channel with your colleagues.

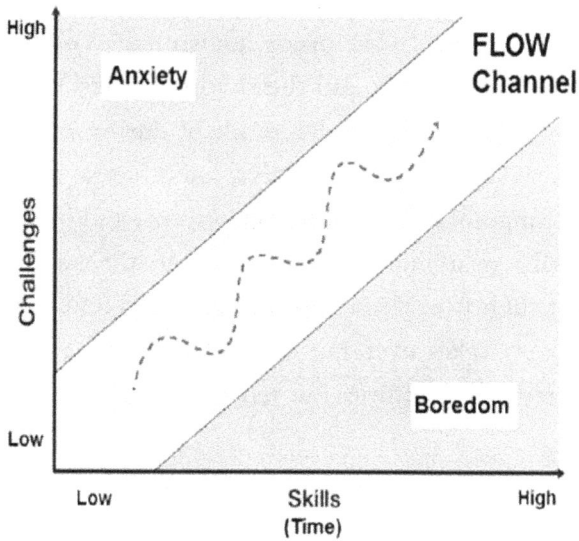

For SLTs, the outcome of being in flow as a team translates into sharper strategy sessions, faster pivots during crises, quicker decision-making and a healthy performance culture. However, the reality is often very different, with ego, politics, pressure, complexity and competing priorities all conspiring to disrupt the conditions needed for flow.

Creating the right conditions for flow within an SLT does not happen by chance. It requires intentionality at both the individual and team level. Flow thrives on clarity. Vague objectives scatter attention and create confusion, both of which are fatal to flow. For senior teams, clear goals mean agreeing not only on what needs to happen, but also why it matters and how success will be judged.

Teams in flow continually receive signals about their performance – what is working and what needs adjustment. Without real-time feedback, uncertainty grows and the rhythm breaks. Often, this does not require a formal check-in. More likely, during a conversation, it just takes a raised eyebrow or a quizzical look that says, *Are we together on this?* Anything unclear? Confidence returns, and people re-engage with the challenge at hand. Flow occurs in the sweet spot where challenge just slightly exceeds skill. Too easy, and boredom sets in; too hard, and anxiety takes over. For senior teams, this means designing work that stretches capabilities but remains achievable.

Staying in flow demands deep focus. Disruptions – whether from emails, phones or side conversations – fracture attention and make it almost impossible to sustain a flow. Leaders must be deliberate in protecting critical sessions from external intrusions. At every workshop I facilitate, I bring a storage unit for mobile devices. I simply say, "rack 'em and stack 'em," and everyone knows to turn their phone to silent and hand it over. It is simple, yet highly effective in setting the mood for the challenge at hand.

People can only lose themselves in the task when they are not self-censoring out of fear of failure. Psychological safety – the sense that one can speak up without risk of humiliation or retribution – is essential for team flow. It is OK not to know. Teams in flow feel deeply connected, not just to the task but to each other. High-trust teams can move faster and debate more fiercely because they instinctively understand the dynamics of constructive conflict and how it results in clearer outcomes and stronger commitment through co-creation.

Just as fatigue, stress and burnout are flow killers, flow is highly sensitive to interpersonal tensions. Minor resentments, unspoken grievances or competing agendas will eventually surface and fracture team unity. Leaders must manage their own energy levels, while regular 1-2-1s help keep individuals "match fit." It is often the case that an individual may start to underperform as a firm grows or scales beyond their capabilities. Such situations cannot be swept under the carpet and must be addressed either through coaching or by having an honest conversation about alternative futures.

Senior leadership teams today face volatile, uncertain, complex and ambiguous (VUCA) environments. Achieving and maintaining a state of flow offers not only a performance edge but also a profound shift in how teams experience their work. It replaces grind with engagement, perspiration with inspiration and anxiety with a sense of powerful progress.

The SLT is the engine room of any organisation, steering both daily operations and long-term strategic direction. Its effectiveness hinges not just on the capabilities of individual members, but on how well they collaborate, communicate and prioritise together during the working week.

Time Management

A foundational discipline for any SLT leader is the ability to distinguish between what is important and what is urgent. Stephen Covey's description of the Eisenhower time management matrix is a helpful approach that categorises tasks into four quadrants.[9] The matrix's structure provides a framework for understanding common time management challenges:

Quadrant I (Urgent and Important). Tasks that require immediate attention, such as crises and pressing problems

Quadrant II (Important but Not Urgent). Activities that are crucial for long-term success, like strategic planning and relationship building.

Quadrant III (Urgent but Not Important). Tasks that demand immediate attention but may not contribute significantly to long-term goals, such as certain meetings or interruptions.

Quadrant IV (Not Urgent and Not Important). Activities that offer minimal value and can often be eliminated.

SLT leaders frequently complain about how they find themselves reacting to urgent tasks (Quadrants I and III), potentially at the expense of strategic activities in Quadrant II.

	Urgent	**Not Urgent**
Important	**1.** **Necessity** (Manage) • Pressing problems • Crisis • Rush deadlines • Re-working ✓ **Do**	**2.** **Productivity** (Focus) • Strategy and planning • Project planning • Risk management • Personal development ◓ **Decide & Schedule**
Not Important	**3.** **Distraction** (Automate) • Interruptions • Email /phone calls • Administrative tasks • Social media posting ↓ **Delegate**	**4.** **Waste** (Eliminate) • Trivia • Internet surfing • "Busyness" • Escape activities ✗ **Delete**

The UK-based Development Academy conducted research in 2021 with 500 individuals across various industries, finding that the Eisenhower Matrix is the most effective time management strategy. Half of those who use this technique report that their work is under control every day, and 50% say it is under control four out of five days each week.[10] However, only 2% of individuals were reported as using the Eisenhower Matrix to manage their time.[11] In a nutshell, almost nobody uses it – but those who do find it very effective.

I am always struck, when visiting a new client, by the background hum in the office. If it is noisy at the SLT level, I instinctively know there is work to be done on planning and delegation disciplines. Too often, I meet SLT leaders who are stressed, working long hours and shackled to their desks with "just one more thing to do before we start," while junior and middle managers appear to enjoy a quieter, more relaxed working life. The harsh reality is that they are often acting in a vacuum – second-guessing their leadership.

Research from the British Chamber of Commerce suggests SLT leaders should spend at least 40% of their time in Quadrant 2 – defining and deciding on business strategy, and scheduling time and resources for its execution. The noise and buzz of activity in any office should ideally be nearer the front line, where tasks are completed.

Start and Finish the Week

Effective collaboration depends on how well team members regulate their own emotions and respond to others. SLTs are often made up of high achievers with strong opinions – a strength that requires tact and guile to harness effectively. In many SLTs, the problem is not a lack of talent but a failure to fully channel it. Without EQ, smart people can unintentionally talk past each other, compete for airtime or shut down when they feel unheard.

Practising EQ also demands time. I am an advocate for starting and closing the week with *SLT huddles,* which act as bookends to the working week. These brief, informal check-ins, lasting 15 to 30 minutes, signal a clear break between work life and leisure time. They instinctively utilise the Eisenhower Matrix, which is designed to bring everyone onto the same page at the start of the week and to finish the week together, having accomplished tangible results as a team.

The core purpose of the *start-of-the-week huddle* is to align the leadership team on what matters most right now, with a review of priorities, a traffic-light status update on key initiatives, and the identification of potential issues before they arise. Such huddles make the tactical weekly meeting with the broader team, including department heads, run far more smoothly.

By contrast, the *close-of-the-week huddle*, also no more than 30 minutes, is more reflective and grounded in the principles of continuous improvement. It reviews progress on current priorities, identifies learning and cheers on success:

- How was the week? Did we achieve our stated priorities? What changed, and why?

- What have we learned? Were there successes or failures that offer insights? What should we carry forward?

- Celebration time. What wins should be recognised – both big and small – and which teams or individuals made a difference?

The reflection should not be heavy or punitive. It should be conducted with a light touch, spotlighting learning and acknowledgement. Even in weeks when targets are not fully met, highlighting effort and progress boosts morale. The meeting should always conclude by celebrating success or progress toward goals in growth, innovation and customer impact. Doing so enables the team to adjourn for the weekend with constructive closure on the week's work – and return refreshed for the start of the following one.

By starting and finishing the week with these huddles, effective leaders can effectively use EQ to mitigate the impact of conflicts, clashing priorities and personal rivalries, reframing disagreements as a search for the best solution. Humour is invaluable in such moments – and far from being a distraction from serious work, it is often the gateway to it. Good humour signals: *You're safe here. You can relax. You can be yourself.*

When EQ levels are raised, an SLT does not shy away from hard conversations. Instead, people feel safe. They speak up. They challenge ideas. They admit mistakes. They commit to trying new things. Time and again, I have seen how these short huddles can cut through hours of what would otherwise be bruising debate, helping teams move past interpersonal tensions with some well-timed light-hearted humour – and achieve better solutions.

Flexing Resources for Impact

Managing resourcing challenges is one of the most persistent and vexing challenges facing an SLT, particularly in growing or fast-moving organisations. While short-term contract hiring offers quick fixes, it often comes at the cost of culture dilution, higher expense and missed opportunities for internal growth. Much better to maximise the use and development of long-term staff who can be trained and deployed flexibly across multiple business areas.

Investing time and energy in proactive workforce planning is more effective than reacting to staffing gaps as they arise. Regular quarterly reviews of future resource needs ideally run in tandem with a business strategy, focusing on forecasted skill requirements for the next 6 to 18 months. The assessment includes upcoming projects and new business areas, potential turnover or succession risks, and, in particular, the emerging skills – both in quantity and quality – needed to maintain delivery and competitiveness.

By identifying needs early, the SLT can focus on internal talent development instead of last-minute external hiring. Effective workforce planning reduces the reliance on contractors and builds a workforce that flexes across different parts of the business. This requires intentional investment in cross-skilling, where SLTs can champion initiatives such as:

- Job rotations, which offer employees opportunities to work temporarily in different departments to broaden their skills

- Project-based learning or assigning cross-functional project roles that expose staff to new challenges and knowledge

- Designing structured training programmes that equip employees with adjacent skills beyond their core expertise

Very often, the right people for a role already exist internally, but they are hidden by organisational silos. Proactive workforce planning includes:

- Maintaining a regular update on the talent inventory that captures employee skills, experiences and aspirations

- Consider offering vacancies to current staff first before going out to market

- Encourage managers to nominate high-potential employees for stretch opportunities across teams

By making talent more visible and mobile, the SLT further reduces the need for short-term external hires while boosting employee retention.

Managing Change vs Delivering Business as Usual (BAU)

Balancing change with continuity is arguably the most enduring tension in business. The SLT holds a dual mandate: accountability for delivering results today while also acting as architects of the future. Meeting both demands requires conscious leadership. Strategic foresight must be coupled with operational discipline.

SLTs that thrive on this balancing act establish routines that protect time for long-range thinking, while maintaining a sharp focus on present outcomes. They use data to prioritise, resist the pull of urgent-but-unimportant activity and model leadership behaviours that encourage others to do the same.

The most effective SLTs regularly zoom in and out – clarifying long-term direction while also supporting the people, processes and systems needed to deliver in the present. Rather than toggling between "now" and "next," they treat both as interconnected domains of leadership and strategy, ensuring that the short term is managed in service of a sustainable and bold future.

One way to approach this challenge is through tools such as McKinsey's *Three Horizons Model*, which helps SLTs map current initiatives while simultaneously envisioning transformative growth.[12]

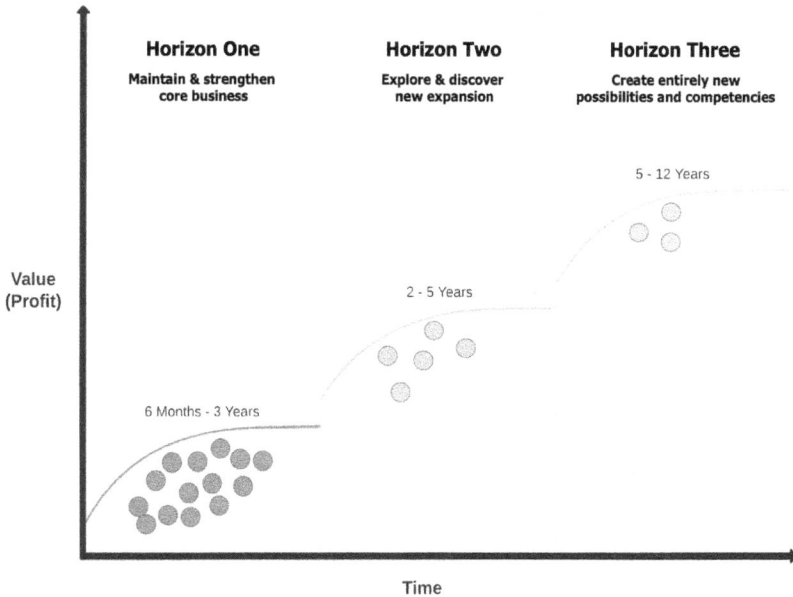

On the operational side, SLTs adopt prioritisation tools such as OKRs (see Chapter 7) or balanced scorecards to maintain alignment between near-term delivery and long-term ambition. Cadence is also critical, ensuring time is set aside for strategic conversations rather than being consumed by operational updates. Off-sites, quarterly strategy reviews, robust S&OP processes and proactive workforce planning create the space to work *on* the business, not just *in* it.

Summary

At the heart of every highly effective SLT lies a paradox: the same diversity of expertise, perspective and ambition that gives a team its power is also the source of its greatest tensions. This chapter explores five recurrent sources of conflict in SLTs – strategic direction, role clarity, power dynamics, communication and information sharing, and personal values and leadership styles – and demonstrates how, when addressed deliberately, they can become catalysts for collective performance, decision quality and long-term value creation.

Strategic Direction and Priorities

Misalignment in strategic direction often manifests as conflicting priorities, siloed initiatives or inconsistent messaging to the wider organisation. Teams that operate without shared agreement on "where we're going and why" become reactive and fragmented. The antidote is structured, recurring strategy dialogues where the SLT jointly reviews market shifts, long-range goals and near-term pressures. A practical tool here is the Eisenhower Matrix, which is used collectively to distinguish between urgent and important tasks, enabling the team to allocate its focus where it matters most. This promotes deliberate trade-offs between short-term delivery and long-term investment.

Role Clarity and Accountability

When leadership roles blur, decision-making slows down and accountability evaporates. Many SLTs suffer from overlapping mandates or ambiguous leadership on cross-functional issues. Establishing clarity around "who leads on what" – without diminishing collective ownership – is crucial. Teams that routinely map decision rights, shared responsibilities and leadership boundaries reduce duplication and boost speed. Regular use of Monday and Friday SLT huddles can reinforce this clarity: starting the week with aligned intentions and closing it by reviewing key outcomes and learnings.

Power Dynamics and Influence

Unspoken power struggles between founders and new leaders, between functions or across hierarchy can erode trust and transparency. Mature SLTs develop psychological safety and norms that enable open disagreement without political cost. This includes creating space for dissent, rotating meeting chairs to flatten hierarchy and adopting explicit "challenge and support" protocols in decision-making forums. Power becomes less about position and more about contribution.

Communication and Information Sharing

In many SLTs, the left hand often does not know what the right hand is doing. Critical updates may remain siloed within functions, leading to either over-centralised or disjointed decision-making. High-performing SLTs counter this by establishing clear and consistent communication rhythms: shared dashboards, structured updates in huddles and explicit agreements on what should be escalated, shared or decided collectively. The aim is not more communication, but smarter communication, focused on the right people, with the right information, at the right time.

Both formal and informal channels should be in place. SLT WhatsApp or Teams groups, email distribution lists and shared calendars help ensure no one is left out of the loop. Leaders must also stay mindful when subsets of the SLT travel together. Decisions made on the move should be cascaded promptly to the wider team to maintain transparency, alignment and trust.

Personal Values and Leadership Styles

Underlying many SLT tensions are deep differences in values, temperament and leadership philosophy. What one leader sees as a healthy challenge, another interprets as disloyalty. Teams that thrive do not avoid these differences – they surface and explore them. Through structured conversations, personal leadership profiles and feedback loops, SLTs build collective self-awareness and empathy. Over time, this enables cognitive diversity to become a strength, not a fault line.

When SLTs address these conflicts head-on with structure, curiosity and shared purpose, they unlock a state of *team flow*. This is more than cohesion or harmony; it is a rhythm of collaboration where the team feels energised, challenged and connected in pursuit of something bigger than any one individual.

The Eisenhower Matrix operates as a strategic lens, not just a time management tool. SLT huddles become a cultural ritual that reinforces focus, accountability and learning. Resource allocation, once viewed as a battleground, becomes a shared responsibility – with the SLT deliberately managing the tension between running the business today and building it for tomorrow.

This is the essence of high-impact leadership: not the absence of conflict, but the ability to come together to transform friction into *flow.* By combining disciplined tools, clear rhythms and a commitment to conscious leadership, SLTs create a system that enables them to honour the demands of the present while shaping the organisation's future.

A well-functioning SLT is a collective of skilled individuals aligned to a shared mission, operating with discipline, trust and strategic intent. By embedding strong working practices, clearly delineating roles, maintaining a laser focus on priorities and nurturing both performance and wellbeing, the SLT becomes not just a decision-making group but a force multiplier for the entire organisation.

Reflective Questions

The questions set out below are designed to help you internalise key ideas, examine your own experiences in light of what you've read and consider how any insights might shape your thinking and actions in future. There are no right answers – only honest ones. Use these opportunities to reflect, deepen your awareness, spark conversation with others or simply increase awareness of what is changing for you as you work through this book.

How effectively do we strike a balance between long-term ambition and short-term execution?

Are we transparent and timely in sharing relevant information with each other?

Are there unspoken value clashes that show up in decision-making or behaviours?

Do we begin and end our weeks with clarity, focus and alignment?

Do we clearly distinguish between change initiatives and "business as usual"?

There is a longer list of questions in the "Appendix: Reflective Questions." These are designed to be addressed when you, with or without the team, have more time available for reflection, rather than reaction.

Conclusion

"In my teams, the goalie is the first attacker,
and the striker is the first defender."
– Johann Cruyff, footballer and architect of "Total Football'

Cruyff's "Total Football" was not just a tactical breakthrough; it was a radical rethinking of what it means to play as a team. Every player understood the whole, adapted in real-time, assumed collective responsibility and contributed far beyond their traditional role. The same principles are true of exceptional senior leadership teams (SLTs). At their best, they work seamlessly and adaptively, excelling in their roles and responsibilities while effortlessly shifting between strategic thinking and execution. This book serves as a blueprint for building and leading SLTs that perform at the highest level.

Too often, businesses attempt to scale by adding complexity: more roles, more layers and more processes – without strengthening the connective tissue of team leadership. This book offers a different path and describes how to transform SLTs from hierarchical committees into collaborative engines of performance, clarity and cohesion. Drawing on frameworks, behavioural insights, lived experience and disciplined execution, it shows how leaders can unlock the energy, alignment and focus needed to thrive.

Build the Foundations, and Make Them Live

High-performing SLTs rest on three core pillars: shared goals, clear roles and established behavioural norms. Shared goals define what success looks like. Clear roles remove ambiguity and reduce friction. Behavioural norms, intentionally shaped, determine how decisions are made, conflict is handled and collaboration happens. But alignment on these alone is not enough. The real power of an SLT lies in cultivating a positive and purposeful culture that translates strategy into coordinated action by turning big decisions into consistent execution. Execution is the ultimate test of leadership.

This is where the book goes deeper. Strategy is not viewed as a static document or a one-off planning exercise, but as a dynamic, lived and co-created process. For high-performing SLTs, strategy evolves continuously – shaped by real-time learning, cross-functional input and shifting market conditions. The SLT brings strategy to life through a deliberate rhythm of work, characterised by regular touchpoints, strategic reviews and decision-making forums that keep teams aligned and focused. This cadence reinforces priorities, drives accountability and ensures that strategic intent is translated into daily action across the organisation.

By treating strategy as a shared responsibility rather than a top-down directive, SLTs foster ownership at every level. This collaborative approach not only sharpens execution but also creates the agility to adapt quickly when conditions change, ensuring the business remains responsive, resilient and forward-looking.

The leadership blueprint combines visionary thinking with disciplined execution, encouraging innovation while strengthening resilience in organisational structure, processes and ways of working, as well as building both individual and team capabilities.

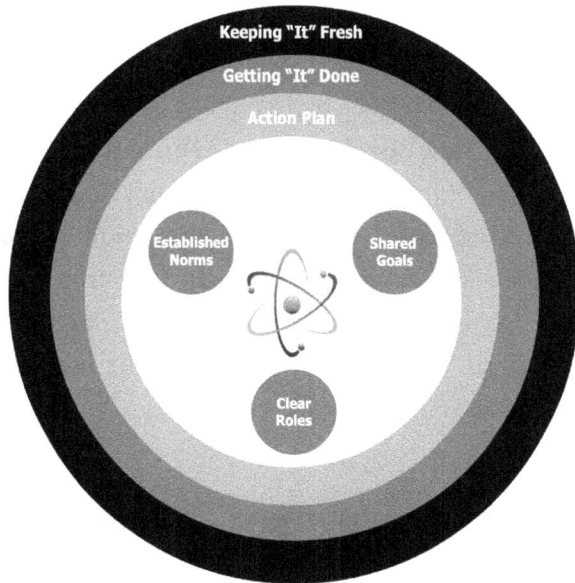

Real-World Lessons, Real-World Impact

Every SLT's starting challenge is bringing the right people into the room with the right mindset. Onboarding is not just about induction materials; it's about acclimating new leaders to the team's norms, building trust and giving people the psychological safety to contribute fully. Deep human connection is not a soft add-on – it's the foundation of high performance.

A recently promoted MD once told me, "I've never seen my SLT this animated, and we didn't even get to the agenda!" We had spent the session mapping personal stories and patterns of conflict. That conversation shifted more in three hours than in six months of reviews. It was a reminder: Human connection is not a side issue – it is the work.

This book also argues that happiness is not a distraction from performance – it is a strategy for it. Teams that feel supported, respected and trusted are more creative, more resilient and more committed. Leading such teams requires intention. It means moving from a command-and-control style to a more empowering one by asking better questions, inviting ownership and modelling curiosity. This shift demands more of senior leaders, but it yields more too: trust, energy and accountability.

A System for Leadership That Scales

This book goes beyond theory to offer a scalable management system, built around four interconnected disciplines:

Strategy – co-created, tested and actively lived

Structure – clear decision rights, role clarity and enabling architecture

Human Connection – trust, safety and truth-telling without fear

Execution Rhythm – feedback loops, OKRs and meeting cadence that drive aligned action

Exceptional SLTs are built on versatility, shared understanding and a clear sense of purpose. Everyone knows the plan. Everyone plays their part. Everyone is ready to step up when needed. Leadership is not about being the hero in your department – it's about leading the business, together.

Once a team is energised, it needs a structure that supports it. Many organisations fall into the trap of mismatching ambition with leadership bandwidth, resulting in decision bottlenecks, overreach or missed targets. Structure must enable strategy. It must be clear who decides what, how accountability flows and where information travels.

OKRs, used well, help turn direction into delivery. They are not a Silicon Valley gimmick. When integrated into the heartbeat of the business – its weekly, monthly and quarterly meetings, as well as in its 1-2-1s – OKRs help close the knowing–doing gap that plagues and derails strategic execution. The secret sauce? Make feedback loops short, visible and mutual so that the SLT can hold each other accountable, learn quickly and adjust rapidly.

I remember working with a technology founder who said, "The problem isn't the plan, it's getting the leadership team to run at the same speed." Over the course of 12 months, we established shared goals, codified team norms and installed a regular execution rhythm. Within two quarters, decision-making accelerated, team friction decreased and customer satisfaction increased by 30%. The plan had not changed, but the team had.

From Good Intentions to Great Execution

The central tension for every SLT is how to deliver today while building for tomorrow. Most teams overcorrect in one direction, either "fighting fires" or living in the future. The real skill is learning to manage that tension, surfacing it and using it as creative friction that sharpens focus and choices.

SLTs that lead well become the spine of the business. They create direction, accelerate decision-making and empower people to grow. They bridge silos and create alignment. They shape culture through what they model and how they show up. And when they work well, everything happens with more energised engagement, execution and innovation.

Lighting the Blue Touch Paper is a manifesto for how SLTs become engines of energy, clarity and performance. It provides the practical and philosophical tools for MDs and senior leaders who want to build teams that truly lead together and inspire others to achieve more. By weaving together strategy, structure, human connection and execution discipline, *Lighting the Blue Touch Paper* provides the blueprint for senior teams looking not just to cope with the accelerating pace of change in a volatile, uncertain, complex and ambiguous world, but to thrive in it.

Ignition Tools

Reading about leadership, strategy and team performance is only the first step.

A lasting impact comes from taking action: testing ideas, reflecting honestly and applying what you've learned. The Ignition Tools help you spark that action, turning key concepts from this book into tangible results and meaningful progress.

These tools are not passive checklists. They are designed for engagement with the senior team and are best supported with the input and guidance of an independent facilitator. Whether it's identifying hidden obstacles that slow your business growth, assessing how well your senior leadership team works together or reflecting on your own leadership presence, the Ignition Tools provide you with the structure, metrics and guidance to act quickly and decisively.

Built for collaboration, the tools allow senior teams to score, compare, and discuss results, turning insights into a shared understanding and measurable progress.

The Ignition Tools live online, making them easy to access from anywhere. You can complete assessments in just a few minutes, receive instant feedback and even visualise results in ways that highlight strengths, gaps and opportunities for improvement. Think of them as the spark that turns the ideas in this book into real, measurable outcomes.

To explore these tools and ignite personal and business growth, access the Ignition Tools here:

<u>www.20-20management.com/ignitiontools</u>

Your journey for turning insight into action starts here.

◊ IGNITION TOOLS

Practical, interactive tools to diagnose strategy, measure team health, assess leadership presence, and spark business growth. Work individually or collaboratively to uncover hidden obstacles and take action.

119 Ways to Inject Growth into Your Business

Kick-start growth with 119 practical levers and ideas to remove barriers and seize opportunities.

Explore Ideas →

Business Strategy Scorecard

5-minute assessment to reveal obstacles limiting growth and.get instant, actionable insights.

Take Assessment →

SLT Health Assessment

Measure alignment, trust, accountability, conflict resolution, and leadership behaviours to improve team performance

Assess Team →

Leadership Presence Diagnostic

Evaluate gravitas, communicatioism, authenticity, and influence. Identify gaps and create a visual profile to

Evaluate Leadership →

References

Preface

1. Charles Handy obituary, *The Times*, 17 December 2024. Available at: https://www.thetimes.com/uk/obituaries/article/charles-handy-obituary-corporate-philosopher-and-author-mczk5gm06.

2. S. Bean, 'Majority of new managers are unprepared and unable to manage their teams', *Workplace Insight Magazine*, 29 June 2017. Available at: https://workplaceinsight.net/majority-of-managers-are-unprepared-to-take-on-their-first-management-role/?utm.

Introduction

1. B. Brown, *Dare to Lead: Brave Work, Tough Conversations, Whole Hearts* (London: Vermillion, 2018).

2. J. Collins, *Good to Great: Why Some Companies Make the Leap and Others Don't* (London: Random House Business Books, 2001).

3. P. Drucker, *The Changing World of the Executive: A Scorecard for Management* (London: Routledge, 2013).

4. J. M. Kouzes and B. Z. Posner, *The Leadership Challenge: How to Make Extraordinary Things Happen in Organisations* (Hoboken, NJ: John Wiley & Sons, 2017).

5. P. Lencioni, *The Ideal Team Player: How to Recognise and Cultivate the Three Essential Virtues* (San Francisco: Jossey-Bass, 2016).

6. D. Marquet, *Turn the Ship Around!: A True Story of Turning Followers into Leaders* (London: Portfolio Penguin, 2015).

7. R. Martin and A. G. Lafley, *Playing to Win: How Strategy Really Works* (Boston, MA: Harvard Business Review Press, 2013).

8. J. Maxwell, *The 17 Indisputable Laws of Teamwork: Embrace Them and Empower Your Team* (Nashville, TN: Thomas Nelson, 2003).

9. M. Porter, *Competitive Strategy: Techniques for Analysing Industries and Competitors* (New York: Free Press, Macmillan Publishing, 1980).

10. S. Sinek, *Leaders Eat Last: Why Some Teams Pull Together and Others Don't* (London: Portfolio Penguin, 2014).

11. McKinsey & Company, *High-performing Teams: A Timeless Leadership Topic*, 28 June 2017.

12. D. Rigby and B. Bilodeau, 'No One Knows Your Strategy – Not Even Your Top Leaders', *MIT Sloan Management Review*, 2017. Available at: https://sloanreview.mit.edu/article/no-one-knows-your-strategy-not-even-your-top-leaders/.

13. Center for Creative Leadership, *Are You Getting the Best Out of Your Senior Leadership Team?* (Greensboro, NC: CCL Press, 2020). Available at: https://www.ccl.org/articles/white-papers/getting-best-executive-team/.

14. Bain & Company, 'At the Top, It's All About Teamwork', *Bain Insights*, 2016. Available at: https://www.bain.com/insights/at-the-top-its-all-about-teamwork/.

15. LeadershipIQ, 'How Effective Is Your Executive Leadership Team?', *LeadershipIQ Survey*, 2021. Available at: https://www.leadershipiq.com/blogs/leadershipiq/how-effective-is-your-executive-leadership-team-new-data-reveals-surprising-challenges-for-the-top-management-team.

16. Bain & Company, *How to Make the Most of Executive Team Meetings*, 3 March 2021.

17. McKinsey & Company, *Untangling Your Organisation's Decision Making*, 21 June 2019. Available at: https://www.mckinsey.com/capabilities/people-and-organizational-performance/our-insights/untangling-your-organizations-decision-making?utm.

Chapter 1: The Right Stuff

1. C. Dweck, *Mindset: The New Psychology of Success* (New York: Random House, 2006).

2. F. Cave, *Sower, Grower, Mower* (Lancaster: Lancaster University, 2000).

3. P. Lencioni, *The Five Dysfunctions of a Team: A Leadership Fable* (San Francisco: Jossey-Bass, 2002).

4. T. R. Clark, *The 4 Stages of Psychological Safety: Defining the Path to Inclusion and Innovation* (Oakland, CA: Berrett-Koehler Publishers, 2020).

5. A. C. Edmondson, *The Fearless Organisation: Creating Psychological Safety in the Workplace for Learning, Innovation and Growth* (Hoboken, NJ: John Wiley & Sons, 2018).

6. J. T. Chambers, remarks as Chairman and CEO, Cisco Systems, 2006–2015.

7. G. Wickman, *Traction: Get a Grip on Your Business* (Dallas, TX: BenBella Books, 2012).

Chapter 2: Foundational Alignment

1. P. Lencioni, *The Advantage: Why Organisational Health Trumps Everything Else in Business* (San Francisco: Jossey-Bass, 2012).

Chapter 3: Happiness and Productivity

1. A. J. Oswald, E. Proto and D. Sgroi, 'Happiness and Productivity', *Journal of Labor Economics*, 33(4), 2015, pp. 789–822.

2. S. Achor, *The Happiness Advantage: How a Positive Brain Fuels Success in Work and Life* (New York: Crown Business, 2010).

3. Gallup, *State of the Global Workplace Report* (Washington, DC: Gallup, 2021 and 2025).

4. R. M. Ryan and E. L. Deci, 'Self-determination Theory and the Facilitation of Intrinsic Motivation, Social Development, and Well-being', *American Psychologist*, 55(1), 2000, pp. 68–78.

5. B. L. Fredrickson, 'The Role of Positive Emotions in Positive Psychology: The Broaden-and-Build Theory of Positive Emotions', *American Psychologist*, 56(3), 2002, pp. 218–226.

6. T. M. Amabile, S. G. Barsade, J. S. Mueller and B. M. Staw, 'Affect and Creativity at Work', *Journal of Applied Psychology*, 91(4), 2005, pp. 439–456.

7. E. Seppala and K. Cameron, 'Proof That Positive Work Cultures Are More Productive', *Harvard Business Review*, 2016. Available at: https://hbr.org/2015/12/proof-that-positive-work-cultures-are-more-productive.

8. Society for Human Resource Management (SHRM), *Employee Well-being and Retention Report* (Alexandria, VA: SHRM, 2021).

9. The American Institute of Stress, *The Impact of Stress on Health and Productivity* (Fort Worth, TX: AIS, 2020). Available at: https://www.stress.org.

10. Axa, *Study of Mind and Wellbeing* (Paris: Axa Group, 2023).

11. E. Diener and M. E. Seligman, 'Very Happy People', *Psychological Science*, 13(1), 2002, pp. 81–84.

12. UK Department for Business, Energy & Industrial Strategy, *Employee Well-being in the UK Workplace Report* (London: DBEIS, 2019).

13. T. Hsieh, *Delivering Happiness: A Path to Profits, Passion, and Purpose* (New York: Business Plus, 2010).

14. A. J. Rucci, S. P. Kirn and R. T. Quinn, 'The Employee-Customer-Profit Chain at Sears', *Harvard Business Review*, January–February 1998, pp. 82–97.

Chapter 4: Delegate Authority to Empower and Create Leaders

1. D. Marquet, *Turn the Ship Around!: A True Story of Turning Followers into Leaders* (London: Portfolio Penguin, 2013).

2. D. Marquet, *Leadership Is Language: The Hidden Power of What You Say and What You Don't* (London: Penguin Business, 2020).

3. S. G. Isaksen, *Creative Approaches to Problem Solving: A Framework for Innovation and Change* (Thousand Oaks, CA: SAGE Publications, 2010).

Chapter 5: Set Up for Success

1. E. Jaques, *Requisite Organisation: A Total System for Effective Managerial Organisation and Managerial Leadership for the 21st Century* (Arlington, VA: Cason Hall, 1996).

2. B. Brown, *Dare to Lead: Brave Work, Tough Conversations, Whole Hearts* (London: Vermillion, 2018).

3. J. Roberts, *The Modern Firm: Organisational Design for Performance and Growth* (Oxford: Oxford University Press, 2007).

4. P. Lencioni, *The Five Dysfunctions of a Team: A Leadership Fable* (San Francisco: Jossey-Bass, 2002).

5. N. Machiavelli, *The Prince* (Florence, 1532).

6. W. W. Burke and G. H. Litwin, 'A Causal Model of Organisational Performance and Change', *Journal of Management*, 18(3), 1992, pp. 523–545.

Chapter 6: Strategy for Execution

1. K. Blanchard Organisation (D. Ruhe), 'Good Plans Vs Good Execution: Which Needs the Most Attention?', 2013. Available at: https://www.kenblanchard.com.

2. R. Rumelt, *Good Strategy / Bad Strategy: The Difference and Why It Matters* (London: Profile Books, 2011).

3. R. Martin and A. G. Lafley, *Playing to Win: How Strategy Really Works* (Boston, MA: Harvard Business Review Press, 2013).

4. J. Doerr, *Measure What Matters: OKRs, The Simple Idea That Drives 10X Growth* (London: Portfolio Penguin, 2017).

5. A. Smith, *No Bullshit Strategy* (London: Rethink Press, 2023).

Chapter 7: Closing the Knowing-Doing Gap

1. J. Pfeffer and R. I. Sutton, *The Knowing-Doing Gap: How Smart Companies Turn Knowledge into Action* (Boston, MA: Harvard Business School Press, 1999).

2. J. Gothelf, 'How to Recognise OKRs Masquerading as Strategy', 2025. Available at: https://jeffgothelf.com/blog/okrs-masquerading-as-strategy.

3. Chartered Institute of Personnel and Development (CIPD), *HR Outlook Survey* (London: CIPD, 2017). Available at: https://www.cipd.org.

4. M. Smith, keynote speeches on "Delegation and Grip", *Vistage International*, 2001–2024.

5. Deloitte, '37% Performance Improvement Using OKRs', *Deloitte Insights*, 2024. Available at: https://www2.deloitte.com.

6. Deloitte, '2.5X Greater Revenue Growth with Well-Aligned OKRs', *Deloitte Insights*, 2024. Available at: https://www2.deloitte.com.

7. Google, 'How Google Sets Goals: OKRs / Startup Lab Workshop', *YouTube*, 2013. Available at: https://www.youtube.com/watch?v=mJB83EZtAjc.

Chapter 8: Dance to The Rhythm of Meetings

1. P. Lencioni, *Death by Meeting: A Leadership Fable... About Solving the Most Painful Problem in Business* (San Francisco: Jossey-Bass, 2004).

2. G. Wickman and M. Paton, *Get a Grip: An Entrepreneurial Fable... Your Journey to Get Real, Get Simple, and Get Results* (Dallas, TX: BenBella Books, 2012).

3. D. Gray, S. Brown and J. Macanufo, *Gamestorming: A Playbook for Innovators, Rulebreakers, and Changemakers* (Sebastopol, CA: O'Reilly Media, 2010).

4. L. Constantine, *The Peopleware Papers: Notes on the Human Side of Software* (New York: Dorset House Publishing, 2001).

Chapter 9: Raising the Bar with 1-2-1s

1. Deloitte, *Global Human Capital Trends Report* (New York: Deloitte, 2015). Available at: https://www2.deloitte.com.

2. Gallup, 'Performance Reviews Inspire Improvement?', *Gallup Workplace Study*, 2022. Available at: https://www.gallup.com.

3. R. I. Sutton, 'Why Adobe Killed Off the Annual Performance Review', *LinkedIn*, 2018. Available at: https://www.linkedin.com/pulse/why-adobe-killed-off-annual-performance-review-robert-i-sutton.

4. T. Warren, 'Microsoft Axes Its Controversial Employee-Ranking System', *The Verge*, 2013. Available at: https://www.theverge.com/2013/11/12/5095894/microsoft-axes-employee-ranking-system-stack-ranking.

5. P. Cohan, 'Why Stack Ranking Worked Better at GE Than Microsoft', *Forbes*, 2012. Available at: https://www.forbes.com.

6. Chartered Institute of Personnel and Development (CIPD), *HR Outlook Report* (London: CIPD, 2017). Available at: https://www.cipd.org.

7. J. Whitmore, *Coaching for Performance: The Principles and Practice of Coaching and Leadership* (London: Nicholas Brealey, 1992).

8. K. Scott, *Radical Candor: How to Get What You Want by Saying What You Mean* (London: Pan Macmillan, 2017).

Chapter 10: Winning Practices and Habits

1. Chartered Institute of Personnel and Development (CIPD), *Managing Conflict in the Workplace Report* (London: CIPD, 2021).

2. Advisory, Conciliation and Arbitration Service (ACAS), *Estimating the Costs of Workplace Conflict* (London: ACAS, 2021). Available at: https://www.acas.org.uk.

3. K. M. Eisenhardt, J. L. Kahwajy and L. J. Bourgeois, 'How Management Teams Can Have a Good Fight', *Harvard Business Review*, July–August 1997, pp. 77–85.

4. D. C. Hambrick, 'Top Management Groups: A Conceptual Integration and Reconsideration of the "Team" Label', *Research in Organisational Behavior*, 16, 1994, pp. 171–214.

5. J. R. Katzenbach and D. K. Smith, *The Wisdom of Teams: Creating the High-Performance Organisation* (Boston, MA: Harvard Business School Press, 1993).

6. A. C. Edmondson, 'Psychological Safety and Learning Behaviour in Work Teams', *Administrative Science Quarterly*, 44(2), 1999, pp. 350–383.

7. D. Goleman, 'Leadership That Gets Results', *Harvard Business Review*, March–April 2000, pp. 78–90.

8. M. Csikszentmihalyi, *Flow: The Psychology of Optimal Experience* (New York: Harper Perennial, 2008).

9. S. Covey, *The 7 Habits of Highly Effective People* (New York: Free Press, 1989).

10. Timewatch, 'Research Findings on Use of the Eisenhower Matrix', 2022. Available at: https://www.timewatch.com.

11. Acuity Training, 'Original Research on Eisenhower Matrix', 2025. Available at: https://www.acuitytraining.co.uk

12. McKinsey & Company, 'Enduring Ideas: The Three Horizons of Growth', *McKinsey Insights*, 2009. Available at: https://www.mckinsey.com.

Appendix
Reflective Questions

Make Time to Reflect, Not Just React

The following questions are not designed to be rushed through or answered on instinct. They are an invitation to step out of the day-to-day noise and look honestly at how your organisation is really functioning, from strategy and structure to leadership habits and team dynamics.

Used effectively, these questions are designed to help you delve deeper than a surface-level diagnosis. They enable fresh insight, sharper focus and better choices. Whether you work through them alone or with your team as part of a leadership offsite, they are most valuable when you pause to reflect, discuss openly and challenge assumptions.

Consider setting aside time to focus on one theme at a time. Ask not just, "How are we doing?" but "What's holding us back?" and "What could we do differently that would make a real difference?"

The reward for slowing down to think more deeply is often a faster path to meaningful progress.

Chapter 1: The Right Stuff

Recruitment – Specification

- Can you crisply express the ideal candidate for the SLT role that needs to be filled in a few words?

    - Do you know the questions to ask to be sure you are looking in the right place to find what you are seeking?

- Can you identify the key characteristics that produce exceptional performance from SLT team members in their roles?

    - Where do you need to spend time and attention?

Recruitment - Fit

- What is the specific strategic gap this role is meant to fill?

    - Are you recruiting for that gap, or just replacing a person?

- How will this new leader help drive your vision forward over the next 2 - 3 years?

- What critical decisions will they be expected to shape or lead in their first year?

Recruitment - Team Dynamics & Leadership Contribution

- What does the current SLT gain, or risk, by adding this person?

- Are you looking for someone who will challenge the team, align with it or both?

- How do you want this individual to show up in the room when hard decisions are being made?

Recruitment - Cultural Alignment

- What behaviours and values are non-negotiable for someone joining your SLT?

- In what ways do you want this person to evolve your culture and not just fit into it?

- Where do you anticipate potential points of friction with the existing team, and how will you address them?

Onboarding & Integration

- What does a successful first 90 days look like for this person, not just functionally, but relationally?

- How will you help them build trust quickly across the organisation?

- Who on the team will help integrate them, and who might resist?

  - How will you help overcome resistance?

- What can you do more to be sure you really get the best from your new SLT leaders as they are promoted into the role, or step into the role from outside?

  - What conversations can you initiate to foster stronger and deeper connections within the team?

   ◦ How can you encourage people to be better and build a smarter organisation?

Your Leadership Intent

- As the MD, what do you most need from this person: challenge, loyalty, execution, creativity?

- Where will you need to adapt your own leadership to make space for them to succeed?

- When was the last time you checked you have got "the right people, in the right seats, facing the right way, on the bus?"

  ◦ Where are the gaps, and what needs to be done to address them?

- If a new hire goes really well, what's different in the business a year from now?

  ◦ If it doesn't, what might have gone wrong?

Do They "Get It"?

- Do they demonstrate a clear grasp of their role beyond functional expertise, including their enterprise-wide responsibilities?

- How well do they understand how their work connects to strategy and long-term value creation?

- Are they aware of the dynamics and needs of the broader team, not just their own function or agenda?

- Do they contribute meaningfully to cross-functional discussions and big-picture decision-making?

- Are they quick to identify patterns, risks and opportunities without needing to be directed?

Do They Want It?

- Are they visibly energised by the challenges and responsibilities of their role, or are they just going through the motions?

- Do they take full ownership, or do they wait for permission or direction?

- Do they actively lean into the tough stuff – ambiguity, conflict and trade-offs of leadership?

- Are they present and emotionally invested in the success of the entire team, or are they just protecting their own interests?

- How do they show personal commitment to the organisation's success, even when it's hard or unpopular?

Have They the Capacity to Develop?

- When given feedback, do they reflect, respond and change?

  ○ Or defend and deflect?

- Have they demonstrated growth in any area over the last 6 to 12 months?

- Do they have the humility to admit what they don't know and the curiosity to learn it?

- Are they coaching others and also coachable themselves?

- Do they adapt well to change, or get stuck in old patterns?

Chapter 2: Foundational Alignment

Connection & Trust

- When was the last time we felt truly connected in this team?

  - What contributed to that feeling?

- In a world of "hybrid and remote working," what are we doing to ensure the SLT is bonded as they lead across different locations and time zones?

- Are we able to have open, honest and sometimes difficult conversations without fear of judgment?

- What signals do I get from this team that I am a valued and trusted colleague?

- Are we setting aside time to build relationships and strengthen team trust?

- What assumptions might I be making about others on this team that need checking or rethinking?

- Are we actively listening to each other, or do we default to defensive positions?

- Do I really believe that this is my number 1 team?

Shared Values in Practice

- Can I name the values that we claim to hold as a team?

    - Where do I see these values clearly lived out in our day-to-day work?

- Where is the gap between our stated values and how we operate under pressure?

- How do we hold each other accountable to our shared values, especially when it's difficult?

- When have I compromised on a value, and what was at stake?

- What value or principle do I personally bring to this team that I'd like to see more widely shared?

- Are we setting the right cultural tone for the organisation through our actions and decisions?

Role Clarity

- Do we feel clear on our roles and how they knit into the whole? Where is there ambiguity or overlap?

- What do others think my role is, and how might that differ from my own view?

- What unique strengths or perspectives do we each bring to this team, and do we feel they are fully utilised?

- Where might we be duplicating effort, or leaving gaps, because we're unclear on roles?

- Do we agree on who has the final decision-making authority in key areas?

- What one conversation about roles and responsibilities would help improve how we work together?

Shared Goals

- To what extent do we each understand and agree on the organisation's strategic priorities?

- Are we pulling in the same direction, or do we have competing priorities that pull us apart?

- How do we strike a balance between short-term delivery pressures and long-term strategic goals?

- Where have we seen alignment in action, and where have we felt the absence of it?

- How do we check and recalibrate our shared goals as conditions change?

- Whose voice or perspective might be missing as we define these goals?

- Are we clear on how our individual functions contribute to the organisation's collective outcomes?

SLT Charter

- What does success look like for this leadership team in the next 12–18 months?

- What is the purpose of this leadership team, beyond our functional responsibilities?

- What commitments are we willing to make to each other, and to the broader organisation?

- What behaviours do we want to model, regardless of pressure or circumstance?

- How will we make decisions, especially when we do not all agree?

- What norms do we want to establish around communication, feedback and accountability?

- How do we want to handle conflict or tension when it inevitably arises?

- What does trust look like in this team, and what might threaten it?

- What will we measure to hold ourselves accountable as a leadership team, not just as individuals?

Operational Alignment

- Are we aligned on the strategic priorities for the next 12 to 24 months?

- Are we consistently communicating the same message to our teams?

- Do we trust each other's intentions, capabilities and decisions?

- Do we support each other publicly and address disagreements privately?

- Are we acting as a cohesive unit, or are we operating in silos?

- Do we support and challenge each other in a balanced way?

Chapter 3: Happiness and Productivity

Psychological Safety & Trust

- Do people in our organisation feel safe to speak up, challenge ideas or admit mistakes without fear of blame or judgment?

- What signals, explicit or subtle, do we give that build or erode trust within the team?

- How do I respond to feedback or bad news, and what does that teach others about what's safe to share?

Work-Life Balance & Flexibility

- Are we role-modelling healthy boundaries around availability and workload or unintentionally reinforcing overwork?

- Where can we offer more genuine flexibility without compromising performance?

- How do we create space for different definitions of balance, depending on life stage, role or circumstance?

Recognition & Achievement

- Are employees regularly recognised for their contributions in meaningful ways?

- When was the last time I gave meaningful recognition to someone outside my immediate team?

- Do we celebrate outcomes alone, or also the effort, learning and collaboration it took to get there?

- Are our recognition systems inclusive, or do they unintentionally favour certain roles, personalities or working styles?

Development & Growth

- Do all employees have a clear line of sight to growth opportunities, beyond just the "high performers"?

- How often do we talk about career development in ways that go beyond formal training or promotions?

- Are we actively investing in the future potential of my people, or just filling today's gaps?

Social Connection

- How well do we know the people we lead and what matters to them?

- What spaces, formal or informal, exist for people to connect beyond tasks, and how inclusive are those spaces?

- What gets in the way of genuine human connection in our culture, and what could we change?

Health & Well-Being

- Are we proactive about well-being, or mostly reactive when issues arise?

- What pressures are we placing on people, intentionally or not, that may be undermining their health?

- Do our leaders feel empowered and supported to prioritise their own well-being?

Purpose & Meaning

- How clearly have we articulated why we do what we do, and how often do we connect day-to-day work to that purpose?

- Do our people see how their contributions matter, regardless of role or level?

- How do we, as an SLT, personally express our purpose in leadership, and is it resonating with others?

Diversity & Inclusion

- Whose voices are not being heard or represented in key decisions, and what are we doing about it?

- Is our workplace truly inclusive, or just diverse in appearance?

- How do we show through action that belonging matters just as much as performance?

Employee Engagement

- Are we explicitly prioritising employee engagement and satisfaction in our strategic goals?

- How do we measure and track employee engagement, and are we taking action based on the insights uncovered?

- How well do we model the behaviours and values that promote a culture of engagement and well-being?

- Are we consciously addressing toxic behaviours or processes that negatively impact employee morale?

- Are we measuring how employee engagement translates into better customer service and business performance?

Chapter 4: Delegate Authority to Empower and Create Leaders

Intentional Leadership & Delegated Decision-Making

- What decisions are we still holding onto that could be more effectively made closer to the action?

- Do we truly trust people at every level to make good decisions, or do we merely claim to do so?

- Are our expectations and desired outcomes clearly communicated when delegating tasks?

    ○ Do we lead with intent?

- o Do we stop to ask what others recommend we do?

- How do we distinguish between the need for control and the need for clarity?

- Are we creating an environment that encourages initiative and decision-making among employees?

  - o Do we reflect on and learn from the outcomes of delegation to improve our leadership practices?

Empowerment & Ownership at All Levels

- Where are we creating space for people to step up, and where are we accidentally stepping in?

  - o Do we get any pushback on micro-management?

- Do we understand our team members' skills and provide opportunities that align with their strengths and development goals?

- How do we provide the necessary support and resources for our teams to succeed in their delegated tasks?

  - o Do we experience "sand in the gearbox" and become slowly stuck because people lack skills and training

- Do our managers know what "empowerment" looks like in action?

  - o Have we equipped them to lead that way?

- How do I personally respond when someone takes initiative, even if the result isn't perfect?

- What message do we send about ownership, i.e. that it's earned, granted or assumed?

- How do we rate at giving feedback?

  - When we ask for feedback, does accountability silently shift back to resting on our shoulders?

Shared Creative Problem-Solving as Organisational DNA

- Have we agreed what "good problem solving" looks like, and are we modelling it consistently at the top?

- What common language or framework could unite teams across functions and levels when facing complex challenges?

- How do we respond when people raise problems without clear solutions?

  - Do we invite exploration or shut it down?

- What would change in our culture if creative problem-solving became everyone's job, not just leadership's?

Chapter 5: Set up for Success

Strategic Alignment

- How well does our current structure support the delivery of our strategic priorities?

- Where is there misalignment between what we say we value and how we organise to deliver it?

- Are the most strategically important parts of the business positioned with the right influence, visibility and resources?

- Are we structured to serve our current customers, or our future ones?

- What aspects of our strategy are most at risk due to the way we are currently organised?

Operational Efficiency

- Where are the friction points in how work flows across the business?

- How many layers does a decision or action need to pass through?

    ◦ Could we simplify?

- Are we duplicating effort, reinventing the wheel or wasting resources in any part of the structure?

- How easy is it to get things done across teams, departments or functions?

- Where do we experience delays or bottlenecks due to the way we're organised?

People & Talent

- Do people understand their roles, responsibilities and decision-making authority?

- Are we maximising the talent we have, or is it being underutilised in the wrong part of the organisation?

- Where do we see confusion, conflict or misalignment between teams?

- How well does our structure support leadership development and succession?

- What organisational structures are helping, or hindering, people's engagement and motivation?

Scalability & Adaptability

- How quickly could we adapt our structure if the market shifted or growth accelerated?

- Are we overly reliant on a few key people, roles or teams?

- What about our structure makes it hard to innovate, experiment or change direction?

- Do we have a structure that scales with growth, or one that adds complexity as we grow?

- Where are we already seeing signals that the structure is becoming a constraint?

Performance & Results

- Where is performance strongest, and how might structure be contributing?

- Where is performance weak or inconsistent, and how might structure be a root cause?

- Are accountabilities clear enough to drive ownership of results?

- Do our structural boundaries help or hinder our ability to measure and manage performance?

- How often are we surprised by poor results, and is that due to gaps in line of sight or accountability?

- When was the last time we evaluated our structure?

Chapter 6: Strategy for Execution

Cohesiveness of the Strategy

- Do all the parts of our strategy – vision, mission, values, goals and key initiatives – tell a consistent story?

- Can each member of the SLT clearly articulate the strategy in the same way?

- Have we identified and resolved any contradictions or overlaps between strategic priorities?

- Does each member of the SLT organise their own teams to deliver the strategy in collaboration, and in concert, with the rest of the organisation?

- Is the strategy bold enough to inspire, but focused enough to execute?

Organisational Alignment

- Do we understand and agree on the role each organisation unit plays in delivering the strategy?

- Are there any critical interdependencies between departments that haven't been addressed?

- Have we ensured joint ownership of cross-functional initiatives, rather than leaving them in "no man's land"?

- Do our functional plans and capabilities align with the strategic ambitions we've outlined?

Linking Vision to Action

- Can we draw a clear line from our long-term vision to specific strategic goals (annual objectives) and the initiatives we undertake?

- Have we translated strategic goals into measurable outcomes that teams can act on?

- Do we have a management execution system that supports the delivery of strategic goals on a weekly, monthly and quarterly timeline?

- Does everyone – from SLT to "front line" – understand how their work contributes to the strategy?

Practicality and Executability

- Have we been realistic about our resource constraints (people, time, budget, systems)?

- Do we have the operating model and infrastructure to deliver what we're aiming for?

- Have we stress-tested the plan against different scenarios and risks?

- Do our strategic scorecard, KPIs and regular reviews provide us with the right signals to adapt quickly if needed?

Communication Cascade

- Do we stress-test our messages with function /department heads before rolling them out enterprise-wide?

- Are our town halls genuinely two-way?

  - Do we create space for challenge, feedback and honest dialogue?

- How do we measure whether people have understood and are connected with the strategy?

- How do we provide remote, shift-based or non-desk workers with the same level of access and understanding?

- Are our SLT videos human and authentic – or overly scripted and corporate?

- Do our materials demonstrate alignment, shared ownership and passion from the entire SLT?

- Are our visual elements inspiring and helping to tell a story, or are they just decorative?

- Do we recognise and share stories of people who embody our values while driving strategic outcomes?

Chapter 7: Crossing the Knowing-Doing Gap

Management Execution System – Alignment & Structure

- Do we have a clear and shared understanding of our strategic priorities and how they translate into actionable objectives across the organisation?

- Are we using a consistent framework (e.g. OKRs) to cascade objectives and measure progress across teams and individuals?

- How do we ensure visibility and transparency of goals, progress and outcomes at every level of the organisation?

- Is our management execution system agile enough to adapt when priorities shift or challenges emerge?

- Do our operating rhythms, meetings, check-ins and reporting cycles support timely decision-making and continuous alignment?

Effective Delegation – Clarity, Ownership & Support

- Do managers clearly communicate the scope, desired outcomes and boundaries (including time, resources and quality standards) when delegating tasks?

- Are we matching task complexity with the competency and development level of the individual receiving the delegation?

- How do we ensure that delegation does not become abdication, or alternatively, micromanagement?

- Are there feedback loops in place so that delegated tasks are reviewed constructively and supportively?

- Do we train and support managers to develop the judgment necessary to delegate effectively while striking a balance between control and empowerment?

Performance Culture – Expectations, Accountability and Feedback

- Have we clearly defined what high performance looks like in terms of both outcomes and behaviours?

- Is accountability embedded into our performance processes, and do employees understand how their work contributes to broader goals?

- Are our feedback mechanisms regular, two-way, growth-oriented and actioned?

- Do we recognise both the achievement of results and the demonstration of values-driven behaviours in performance conversations?

Reward and Recognition – Reinforcement of the Right Behaviours

- Do our reward and recognition systems reinforce the values, behaviours and results that define our performance culture?

- Are both formal and informal recognition practices actively encouraged and consistently used by leaders at all levels?

- Is recognition timely, specific and meaningful to the recipient?

- Do we measure the impact of reward and recognition on engagement, motivation and performance outcomes?

- Are peer-to-peer recognition and cross-functional collaboration encouraged and rewarded in an appropriate manner?

Leadership Role Modelling – Tone from the Top

- Do SLT leaders model the behaviours we expect from others (e.g. setting clear expectations), giving recognition and holding others accountable?

- Are we, as leaders, visible and seen as approachable, supportive and consistent in reinforcing performance culture principles?

- How do we demonstrate, through our own work and interactions, the value of delegation, collaboration and recognition?

Chapter 8: Dance to the Rhythm of Meetings

Strategic Alignment

- Do our meetings establish a clear line of sight between the company's strategy, OKRs and daily execution?

  - Is it clear how each meeting supports achieving our top priorities?

- Are we using the right meetings to track and drive progress on our strategic goals?

  - Or are we having strategic conversations in tactical meetings?

- Do we have a structured rhythm – daily, weekly, monthly, quarterly or annually – that aligns decisions with the right level of planning horizon?

  - Or are we constantly mixing short-term firefighting with long-term planning?

Meeting Coverage & Structure

- Do we have the right set of recurring meetings at each level of the business: executive, functional, cross-functional and project?

- Do we have a clear purpose for each meeting, and is it still valid?

  - Should we kill, combine or redesign any meetings?

- Is there clarity about which meetings are for decision-making, which are for alignment and which are for sharing updates?

- Do cross-functional teams have enough space to raise risks, align on shared goals and escalate decisions quickly?

Cadence & Flow

- Is the current cadence (e.g. weekly vs. monthly) of our meetings fit for purpose?

  - Are we meeting too often, too little or at the wrong moments?

- Is there a logical flow from one layer of meetings to the next?

○ Do functional reviews inform leadership meetings, and do those outcomes cascade down clearly?

- Are decisions and follow-ups from meetings tracked, acted upon and revisited in a timely way?

Time & Energy Management

- Are we protecting people's time by ensuring meetings are well-scoped, prepared for and time-boxed?

- Are the right people in the room, and only the right people?

- Are meetings energising, outcome-oriented and adding value or are they draining and repetitive?

Execution Support

- Do our meetings lead to clear ownership, next steps and deadlines or just endless discussion?

- Do team members leave meetings inspired and equipped to take action?

- Do we use meetings to remove blockers and accelerate progress, rather than just reviewing them?

- Are we tracking OKR progress in a way that invites curiosity, learning and accountability?

Feedback & Continuous Improvement

- Do we regularly review and improve our meeting cadence and structure as the business evolves?

- Do we gather feedback from teams on whether leadership meetings help or hinder their work?

- Are we modelling meeting discipline at the SLT level: agenda, preparation, timekeeping, follow-through?

Chapter 9: Raising the Bar with 1-2-1s

Purpose & Intent

- Are 1-2-1s viewed as a strategic leadership tool, or just a check-in over coffee?

- Is the purpose (development, alignment, support or performance?) of each 1-2-1 clear?

- Are the 1-2-1s perceived as valuable and tailored to direct reports?

Consistency & Cadence

- Are 1-2-1s happening regularly and reliably, without cancelling and rescheduling?

- Is there a consistent cadence (weekly, bi-weekly, monthly) that suits the needs of each team member?

Focus & Content

- Is there a balance of operational updates, personal well-being and professional development?

- Do the 1-2-1s help team members link their daily work to wider team or company goals?

- Are the 1-2-1 meetings tracking progress on goals, coaching through challenges and identifying learning opportunities?

Action & Accountability

- Is there follow-through on actions or commitments made during 1-2-1s?

- Do the 1-2-1s help the team track their own actions and progress, not just the leader's?

- At the end, is there clarity on what's next, rather than vague agreements?

Feedback & Development

- Is there meaningful feedback during 1-2-1s, not just praise or correction, but coaching for growth?

- Is "radical candour" being exercised to manage difficult conversations?

- Are 1-2-1 meetings building trust and strengthening connections with each person?

Chapter 10: Winning Practices and Habits

Strategic Direction & Priorities

- Are we aligned on our top 3–5 strategic priorities?

- Do we revisit and recalibrate priorities as external or internal factors shift?

- How effectively do we strike a balance between long-term ambition and short-term execution?

Role Clarity & Accountability

- Are leadership roles clearly defined and well understood across the team?

- Do overlaps or gaps in accountability regularly cause friction or delay?

- Do we hold each other accountable for collective and individual outcomes?

Power Dynamics & Influence

- Is influence within the team based on expertise and value, not hierarchy or politics?

- Are all voices heard equally in key decisions?

- Are there unspoken dynamics that hinder open and balanced discussions?

Communication & Information Sharing

- Are we transparent and timely in sharing relevant information?

- Do we actively listen to understand rather than to respond or defend?

- Do we challenge each other constructively and with respect?

Personal Values & Leadership Styles

- Do we understand and appreciate each other's leadership styles and values?

- Are there unspoken value clashes that show up in decision-making or behaviours?

- Do we model the cultural values we want to see across the organisation?

Team Flow & Collaboration

- Do we experience momentum and ease in working together, or friction and drag?

- What conditions help us reach team flow, and what gets in the way?

- How well do we recover after conflict or setbacks?

Time Management & Strategic Focus

- Are we spending enough time "on the business" versus "in the business"?

- Do our meeting agendas truly reflect what matters most?

- Where are we wasting time on low-value tasks, bottlenecks or indecision?

Weekly SLT Cadence (Start/End-of-Week Huddles)

- Do we begin and end our weeks with clarity, focus and alignment?

- Are our huddles purposeful, well-structured and time-efficient?

- What would make them more energising or impactful?

Flexible Resourcing & Capacity Management

- How effectively do we adapt resources to match shifting priorities?

- Do we make evidence-based decisions about where to scale up or scale back our efforts?

- Are there legacy activities we should stop doing?

Managing Change vs. Business-as-Usual (BAU)

- Do we clearly distinguish between change initiatives and BAU?

- Are we leading change at the right pace, with the right engagement and discipline?

- How effectively can we sustain performance during transformation?

www.ingramcontent.com/pod-product-compliance
Lightning Source LLC
Chambersburg PA
CBHW071326210326
41597CB00015B/1365